C000094597

American
Airlines

SIMON FORTY

PLYMOUTH PRESS

Publishing

First published 1997

ISBN 0 7110 2532 0

Published by Ian Allan Publishing

An imprint of Ian Allan Ltd, Terminal House,
Station Approach, Shepperton, Surrey TW17
8AS.

Printed by Ian Allan Printing Ltd at its works at
Coombelands in Runnymede, England.

Code: 9710/B3

CONTENTS

Front cover: *American Airlines'
Douglas DC-10 and Boeing 727 at
San Juan Airport.* Austin J. Brown

Below: *Originally registered
N308AA, Boeing 737-3A4 was
reregistered N674AA in July 1988. In
1992 it was leased to Southwest and is
no longer on American's inventory.*
Austin J. Brown

Acknowledgements
Thanks to all those who helped with this
project, specifically the AA UK Press
Office, Jonathan and Sandra Forty,
Philip Birtles, Austin Brown, Günter
Endres, Peter March and Leo Marriott.

Introduction

American Airlines is one of the biggest scheduled passenger carriers in the world and has one of the largest fleets in the world. It is owned by the AMR Corporation, whose company headquarters are at Dallas/Fort Worth International Airport, Texas. The Airline Group consists of American's passenger and cargo divisions and AMR Eagle Inc, a subsidiary of AMR.

American Airlines' international operation is supported by a vast domestic network; local feeder services are provided by American Eagle which has four feeder subsidiaries — Executive Airlines, Flagship Airlines, Simmons Airlines and Wings West Airlines. These companies work smaller operations with a connecting turboprop service reaching out into every corner of the United States.

To run this colossal network American employs around 85,000 people, mostly at home in the United States, but also many foreign nationals. It operates a fleet of about 650 aircraft to nearly 200 cities around the world on 2,260 daily flights. American Eagle has a further 1,386 daily flights to 125 regional airports within the United States and the Caribbean, operating from six of American's high-traffic cities.

American's Cargo Division is one of the largest scheduled air freight carriers in the world, with a full range of freight and mail services. In addition, by agreeing co-operative arrangements with other carriers, American Cargo has the ability to transport shipments to virtually every country in the world.

American Airlines had an annual revenue of $16,900 million in 1996, gathered from 80 million passengers and 640,000 tonnes of cargo. In May 1991 American flew its one billionth passenger and acquired invaluable Heathrow landing slots from bankruptcy-threatened TWA.

Below: *N371AA is one of over 40 Boeing 767-323ERs in service with American.*
Austin J. Brown

American had previously been unable to get access into the biggest passenger airport in the world and was consequently denied passage on the most prestigious routes in the world — the transatlantic services from the United States into Heathrow. American made its first scheduled flight into Heathrow in 1991.

Since then the story of American Airlines lies mainly in its phenomenal growth. By summer 1997 American will operate up to 238 nonstop flights a week, on 24 routes from 12 airports in eight countries across Europe to seven US gateway cities. 140 nonstop flights are from the UK alone, operating out of Gatwick, Manchester, Glasgow and Birmingham, as well as Heathrow.

American Airlines' operation spreads even further afield with the help of its code-sharing partners: operators such as British Midland, Gulf Air, Canadian Airlines International, LOT, Qantas, South African Airways and Singapore Airlines, with plans for similar arrangements with China Airlines and El Al.

Currently American Airlines and British Airways are trying to form a broad alliance in the fight for passengers and flights in the cut-throat world of the airline industry. Their plan is to co-ordinate all passenger and cargo services between the United States and Europe, code-sharing on each other's networks as much as possible, and establishing a fully reciprocal, worldwide frequent flier programme. These plans need their respective government's approval, would benefit from the blessing of the European Union, and have to ensure that full anti-trust immunity will be obtained.

This book is too small to cover in anything like enough detail all the myriad operations of the AMR Corporation and so it has concentrated on the core business — American Airlines itself — with only peripheral involvement in the American Eagle or cargo sides. For anyone who wishes to obtain more information on the subject, the American website can be recommended (http://www.amrcorp.com), as can the highly informative pocket timetable.

Below: *Boeing 727-227 N727AA was delivered to Braniff in August 1973 as N421BN. American bought it in January 1981 when it was reregistered. In the background is DC-10-10 N135AA.* Peter R. March

History

American Airlines can trace its long and distinguished history back to within a few short years of the start of commercial air travel. The first regular scheduled flight of what was to become American Airlines was a DH-4 biplane carrying mail between St Louis and Chicago on 15 April 1926. The pilot was Charles Lindbergh, yet to become famous as a pioneer aviator, and at the time chief pilot for the Robertson Corporation. He gathered much of his aviation experience while still a young man flying the mail plane by day and night between St Louis and Chicago regardless of the weather.

The Missouri-based Robertson Aircraft Corporation was founded in 1921, and was the proud holder of the second air mail contract awarded by the US government to private operators under the Kelly Air Mail Act of 1925. However, Robertson was only one of about 85 small companies operating all around the United States that were eventually consolidated into American Airlines. The amalgamation began in 1929 — the year of the great Stock Market crash — when the Aviation Corporation was promulgated as a holding company to buy up and develop other aviation businesses, many of which had popped up using the new aviation technology but which were not viable enough on their own to continue trading profitably. One such was Alaskan Airways, an operating subsidiary working scheduled services in and out of Alaska — even in the late 1920s a fairly remote part of the world. (This subsidiary was sold at a much later date to Pan American World Airways.) The principal companies acquired at this time included Colonial Airways, Interstate Air Lines Inc, Universal Air Lines System, the Embry-Riddle Company and Southern Air Transport. Although these companies were ostensibly bought for their aviation holdings, within the assets of most lay such ancillary businesses as bus operations, radio stations and airport construction firms.

The five principal companies within the Aviation Corporation were constituted as follows:

COLONIAL

Started in 1923 as a charter company called The Bee Line, based at Naugatuck, Connecticut. It tendered for and won the government contract to carry mail over Contract Air Mail Route No 1, Boston–Hartford, Connecticut–New York. Scheduled mail service began on 1 July 1926 and the regular passenger service on 4 April 1927. This is generally accepted to be the first night passenger flight service in the USA. Another Colonial company, Colonial West Airways, inaugurated passenger services in December 1927 between Albany–Rochester–Buffalo–Cleveland, while yet another Colonial company, Canadian Colonial Airways began service the following year between New York-Albany-Montreal.

EMBRY-RIDDLE

A Cincinnati-based company operating since December 1927, Cincinnati-Indianapolis-Chicago.

INTERSTATE AIR LINES INC

Started scheduled services between Atlanta and Chicago in November 1928.

SOUTHERN AIR TRANSPORT

Created from the merger between Texas Air Transport and St Tammany Gulf Coast Airways. Texas Air Transport began scheduled services out of Dallas/Fort Worth in February 1928 and at the same time from other cities around Texas. Three months later, in May 1928, St Tammany started the Atlanta–New

Orleans route, and in January 1929, Houston–New Orleans.

UNIVERSAL

Originally called Continental Air Lines and based in St Louis, the company started a scheduled service between Cleveland-Louisville in August 1928. As an ambitious young company it bought a number of other airlines including Robertson Aircraft operating between Chicago–St Louis, and more importantly, in June 1929, the company merged with the Atchison, Topeka & Santa Fe and New York Central railroads to create the first transcontinental rail and air carrier.

These new additions provided the Aviation Corporation with an erratic, America-wide network of routes and modes of transport, none of which operated with any cohesion and all of which were fiercely protected by their local managers. Furthermore, the aircraft they inherited were an assortment of virtually every flying machine around at the time. Obviously drastic reorganisation was necessary and the decision was made in 1930 to amalgamate all the diverse elements together into one unit — American Airways Inc. Schedules were rationalised and routes re-drawn to eliminate overlaps and duplication, and to make the most of the system. On the ground the administration and management were subjected to the same scrutiny and restructured into a more efficient organisation.

By 1933 American was in a position to order its first designated aircraft, the Curtis Condor. These smart new planes needed

Below: *Many manufacturers tried to make use of their military designs to produce civil aircraft. Here, the Model 39 on test. It had the B-24 Liberator's wing, the PB4Y-2 Privateer's tail and a new fuselage.* Consolidated Vultee via Günter Endres

smart new flight attendants — called stewardesses — to look after the first generation of air passengers. Then, in February the following year, disaster nearly overtook the company when the government cancelled all air mail contracts, removing at a stroke the backbone of the company. It was not to last; happily a few months later new government mail contracts were allocated, and American was able to resume mail runs as before.

Later that year American Airways changed its name to American Airlines Inc and another restructuring took place to create an even better, more integrated route system. Throughout the 1930s the main business of American Airlines remained the air mail services, without which the company would have struggled. Appreciating their vulnerability with such lack of depth, executives within American became convinced that the future of air transport lay in the potentially far more lucrative area of passenger services and set their sights on developing that market. An extension of this increase in air traffic was the danger of mid-air collisions; with the ever increasing numbers of aircraft in the sky, a system of control became vital. American became the pioneer of air traffic control and developed a system which was later universally adopted by all the other airlines and eventually administered and controlled by the American government.

By the mid-1930s passenger demand was on the rise as increasing numbers of people preferred the speed and comfort of air travel to rail or road transport. In September 1934 American introduced the Air Travel Plan, one of the industry's first sales promotion programmes and ultimately the predecessor of today's credit travel. With a public now much more prepared to travel, money was soon pouring into aviation development to exploit the new market and a number of important breakthroughs were made. The Douglas Aircraft Company was at the forefront of

this research and on 1 July 1933 the first DC — Douglas Commercial — flew. Very soon afterwards it reached the open market as the DC-2. American bought a number, but, although they proved good, airworthy aircraft, their passenger carrying capacity was too small to make money for the operators. American engineers looked at the problem and decided that if they could increase the capacity of the Douglas DC-2 from 14 to 21 seats, the company would have an economical basis for passenger service.

Of course, this was not as simple to achieve as it appeared on paper, and far more wholesale changes had to be made before the desired result was achieved. By the time Douglas and American Airlines had finished, they had in effect a new aircraft — the Douglas DC-3, which first flew on 18 December 1935. The engineers had done their job superbly but none could have guessed that the DC-3 would become the yardstick by which all other passenger carrying aircraft would be measured and one of the greatest aircraft ever built. American started DC-3 commercial flights on 25 June 1936 between Chicago and New York. The reliability, ease and comfort of these new aircraft was aggressively promoted by American sales staff and by the end of the 1930s the company was well into profit. It had become the United States' number one domestic air carrier in terms of revenue passenger miles.

When the United States joined the Allies in World War 2, priorities changed. To help the war effort American turned over almost half its fleet to the Air Transport Command and sent along its president, Cyrus Rowlett Smith, who was given the rank of major general and made deputy commander. Air Transport Command was the military airline that operated with logistical support from commercial aircraft and airline pilots. American pilots, crews and engineers went with their planes and operated all round the world. Meanwhile, within the United States, demand for air travel escalated and those staff and fleet left Stateside had their work cut out to cope with the increase. In 1937, on 16 February, American estimated that it carried its one millionth passenger.

CYRUS ROWLETT SMITH

In October 1934, at the age of 34, Cyrus Rowlett Smith became president of American. An aviator with a career stretching back to the early days of Texas Air Transport, Smith rose through the ranks to become vice president and general manager of Southern Air Transport, and then vice president in charge of American Airways' southern division. During the war his aviation and logistical experience was put to service when he was made major general and deputy commander of Air Transport Command. He returned to American Airlines after hostilities ceased and continued as chief executive until early 1968. At this time President Lyndon B. Johnson named him Secretary of Commerce in his administration. However, Smith returned to American again as chairman and chief executive on a temporary basis in 1973 following the resignation of the current chairman, George A. Spater. C. R. Smith died at the age of 90 in 1990.

On 3 July 1993, American Airlines opened the C. R. Smith Museum at Dallas/Fort Worth. The museum celebrates American Airlines' pioneering traditions and numerous contributions to commercial aviation.

In September 1942 American went beyond the borders of the United States for the first time, when it notched up its first international service to two Mexican cities — Monterrey and Mexico City from New York and Dallas/Fort Worth.

With the war still in full swing in 1944, American utilised its considerable mail-carrying expertise to introduce the first domestic scheduled US freight service on 15 October. The trail-blazing flight was made in a Douglas DC-3 carrying high priority material and women's apparel from New York to Los Angeles; meanwhile, another Douglas DC-3 flew east with a cargo of fresh flowers, spinach, aircraft parts and clothing. Demand was good and the business grew; more aircraft were allotted to the cargo-carrying arm — Douglas DC-4s, Douglas DC-6As and Douglas DC-7 freighters were put into service in the 1940s and 1950s. To cope with the increased ground maintenance and quality control checks that the extra aircraft entailed, American established its Tulsa Maintenance and Engineering Base in 1946.

During World War 2 research into commercial aircraft ceased as all development effort went into military planes and technology. However, by the end of the war many of these innovations were applicable to commercial usage; furthermore, the public at large had grown used to the idea of air travel and demand for passenger flights was far greater than ever before. A number of innovative commercial aircraft rolled out of the engineers' hangars: in 1947 American equipped with 50 Douglas DC-6s. These aircraft were fully pressurised and were put to service on sleeper flights between New York and Los Angeles via Chicago, or from other points such as Dallas/Fort Worth. And in 1948, the Convair 240 appeared.

In 1948, after three years of peace and the increase in personal freedom of movement for both jobs and vacations in the United States, American decided to encourage families to fly together. Thus it came up with the Family Fare Plan, designed to enable families to fly together at reduced rates; at the same time American also introduced the scheduled coach service as an economic and comfortable alternative to first class fares.

The last Douglas DC-4 was taken out of American service in 1948 and the last

Above: *The Convair 240 was one of many of the DC-3's intended replacements. NC94219* Flagship Newark, *was delivered in February 1948 and served with American until the end of 1957.* American Airlines via Günter Endres

Below: *The DC-3 was the yardstick against which most piston-engined airliners were measured. It had its origins in an American requirement for a DC-2 sleeper to replace biplanes on its sleeper services. The 'day plane' version was the DC-3.* American Airlines via Günter Endres

Douglas DC-3 was retired in 1949, at which time American was able to proudly boast that it was the only carrier in the United States to fly a completely postwar fleet of pressurised passenger aircraft.

Since the 1930s passengers wanting flight information had to consult vast information boards at flight reservations offices. These display boards showed what seats were available on which flights. With increased air traffic this system became too slow and cumbersome, so it was that in 1952 American introduced the Magnetronic Reservisor; this could tell seat availability of flights and keep track of passengers. Standards of service, too, were constantly being revised, and to get a company-wide standard of dress, deportment and service, American created the first special facility for flight attendant training, the American Airlines Stewardess College. Now called the AA Training and Conference Center, it was built at Dallas/Fort Worth in 1957.

In response to customer desire for quicker coast-to-coast service, in 1953 American pioneered nonstop transcontinental flights in the Douglas DC-7; six years later in January 1959, it introduced the Lockheed Electra, the first turboprop designed in the United States. On 25 January 1959 American began the first transcontinental jet service using new-generation Boeing 707s; the following year it opened its new terminal at New York's John F. Kennedy International Airport, and in 1962 American opened its operation at Chicago's O'Hare International. However, the 707s rapidly became outdated as aviation technology took another leap forward with the introduction of the turbofan engine in 1961, which again American was one of the first airlines to introduce. The following year, in March, American introduced the Convair 990, also powered by fanjets; then in 1964 came the Boeing 727, the first three-engined plane since before the war.

All this time the cargo-carrying arm of American had been steadily growing until by 1964 it was operating Boeing 707 jet freighters; these useful planes could carry 90,000lb (40,860kg) of freight to a 3,000-

Below: *Convair 240 N94235* Flagship Lake Placid *was delivered to American on 30 April 1948 and saw 16 years' of service before being sold in September 1964.* American Airlines via Günter Endres

mile (4,827km) radius. On 5 November 1974, American put into service the first Boeing 747 freighter on domestic routes; these jumbos were capable of a much weightier cargo than their diminutive predecessor — a massive 221,000lb (100,334kg). The 747s were based at New York, Chicago, Los Angeles, San Francisco and Dallas/Fort Worth.

As American updated and refined its fleet with the latest jets, it systematically and concurrently phased out all the piston-powered aircraft. The last such, a Douglas DC-6, was flown by American on 17 December 1966 — the 63rd anniversary of Orville and Wilbur Wright's first successful power-driven flight on 17 December 1903 near Kitty Hawk, North Carolina. The event was commemorated in the first issue of American's in-flight magazine *The American Way* in the Winter 1966/Spring 1967 issue. (The magazine has since been re-christened *American Way*.)

With inter-airline competition getting fiercer all the time, American had to stay at the forefront of technology to keep its customers loyal and entice new fliers. By 1966 American had ordered the wide-bodied Boeing 747 capable of carrying 360 or more passengers. On 5 August 1971 a McDonnell Douglas DC-10 left on its inaugural scheduled flight with American flying from Los Angeles to Chicago. American was the first company to fly the big trijet.

Not far from the United States lie the exotic islands of the Caribbean, a popular holiday destination for Americans and a lucrative market for airline companies to which, until 1970, American had not had access. That year American broke into the competition with a merger with Trans Caribbean Airways and through them acquired valuable slots at the islands' airports. In March 1971 American began flying to Puerto Rico, the US Virgin Islands, Haiti, Curaçao and Aruba. In June 1975 American swapped its transpacific routes with Pan Am for the latter's Caribbean authority, which meant American could start serving Montego Bay and Kingston in Jamaica, Pointe à Pitre in Guadeloupe and

Below: *The DC-7 was a stretched DC-6B, design of which started in 1951. American was first to operate the DC-7, inaugurating non-stop Los Angeles–New York services in November 1953.* American Airlines via Günter Endres

Above: *N394AA was delivered on 17 May 1956. Rendered surplus by the arrival of turboprops and jets, it was converted to a freighter in 1960 continuing in service until sold to Universal in February 1967.* via Günter Endres

Below: *The Boeing 707, the first US commercial jet airliner, flew first on 15 July 1954. American was the first transcontinental user starting New York–Los Angeles services in late January 1959. Here mail is loaded aboard* Flagship Texas *for the overnight flight to LA.* American Airlines via Günter Endres

Above: *The number N7526A was originally allocated to an unbuilt 707-123 and was reallocated to a 707-123B delivered in May 1961. It would serve with American until bought by Tigerair Inc in July 1978.* Ian Allan Library

Below: *American 707s served with distinction until the early 1980s when fuel cost escalation led to the retirement of all 'gas guzzlers'.*
American Airlines via Günter Endres

Above: *The Convair 990 needed costly modifications to get the aircraft anywhere near its designed speed and range. N5605, delivered in 1962, only saw service until 1967.* American Airlines via Günter Endres

Fort de France in Martinique, as well as Montreal in Canada.

In the late 1970s and 1980s trouble in the Middle East sent fuel costs soaring and for the first time the United States suffered a fuel crisis. In common with the automobile, aircraft suffered, as aviation fuel prices reached a premium. As a direct consequence of escalating fuel costs, American decided in 1980 to hasten the retirement of its gas-guzzling Boeing 707 fleet; in January 1981, 26 707s were removed from service and the remaining 36 (including nine 707 freighters) were retired by the end of August. By summer 1981 American was operating six Boeing 747 freighters and all the 707 freighters had been retired.

American could not retire aircraft without replacements and, to hasten the phasing out, placed orders for the Boeing 767 — an aircraft that could carry 200 passengers whilst burning less fuel, at a calculated 35% fuel saving. American ordered 30

transcontinental twin-engined versions in November 1978.

The cargo business was in crisis: the cost of aviation fuel made air freight uneconomic for customers who could turn to road or rail transport as a cheaper alternative. American commissioned a study report and after extensive analysis decided that the freighter fleet should be retired completely and that the company should redirect its cargo into smaller shipments capable of being carried in the holds of its passenger aircraft.

Despite the costs, passengers still wanted to fly, but the competition was fiercer than ever and every minor edge that a company could find for itself was exploited to the maximum. One way to attract customers, was to make pricing the tickets ultra-competitive, buying them as easy as possible, and airport facilities straightforward. So in 1974 American introduced the One-Stop Automated Check-in, and then on 24 April 1977 introduced

Above: *American was joint launch customer for the DC-10, services with the aircraft starting in August 1971 on Los Angeles–Chicago flights. N135AA pictured here was delivered to American in June 1980.* Peter R. March

what the company claims to be the most popular fare in history as well as the first discount fare in the industry — the Super Saver. This offered 35–45% savings on cross-continent flights between New York and California. Such discounting proved an enormous and popular success with the flying public, so American extended the Super Saver ticket in March 1978 to include all the routes, with discounts of between 30 and 50%. These savings were later extended to include flights to neighbouring Canada and Mexico.

These ticketing intiatives produced an appreciable expansion in passenger numbers and the formula has been continued down the years, until in 1985 American were able to offer massive 70% discounts on their Ultimate Super Saver fares. This discounting was designed to compete directly and on equal terms with the cut-rate carriers who were cashing in on the freedom brought about by deregulation.

In the late 1960s and early 1970s,

airlines around the world suffered from an alarming decline in earnings, forcing many of the smaller companies to the brink, and allowing larger carriers to move in on them. The merger between American and Trans Caribbean Airways is a prime example.

The major gap in American services by the late 1970s was the lack of a transatlantic route into the heart of western Europe. American had run a transatlantic service for five years between 1945 and 1950 but had then sold it off. By the late 1970s American wanted a share of these lucrative and popular routes.

In 1982 it opened services to Frankfurt and Paris and, once certificated, operated 767-200ERs on the transatlantic route between Dallas/Fort Worth and Gatwick airport (some 30 miles south of London). New European routes were added in the course of time, but what American needed most was direct access to London Heathrow; it achieved this at last when it eventually acquired TWA's Heathrow slots

Above: *The DC-10-30 is a long-range version of the DC-10 with increased wingspan, more powerful engines and an additional undercarriage leg. Here is N137AA, which American bought from Air New Zealand.* Peter R. March

in May 1991. (See page 22.) But we are jumping ahead of ourselves.

In 1978 the airline industry in general was thrown into chaos when deregulation took place. This removed strict government control over which airline could fly which routes inside the USA and at what price. The immediate effect of the lifting of restrictions was that new markets were there for the taking by the established airlines, but more pertinently, the routes were there also for ambitious new young companies who wanted to get in on the action that they had previously been barred from.

With route restrictions lifted, American was able to fly services to and from airports to which it had previously been unable to get access. Consequently on 20 January 1979 American started a major route expansion: it inaugurated services on 19 new routes to eight new destinations — Albuquerque, Las Vegas, Miami, Minneapolis-St Paul, New Orleans, Reno,

Tampa-St Petersburg and St Maarten. In tandem with this broader approach, American moved its administrative headquarters from the New York metropolitan area to Dallas/Fort Worth. The opportunity was also taken to combine in one complex the training facility known as the Learning Center, and the pilot training facility called the Flight Academy, as well as the Southern Reservations Office.

In 1980 American introduced a service to Nassau in the Bahamas, Guadalajara and Perto Vallarta, Mexico. Then later in the year, on 17 December, it launched a non-stop service between Los Angeles and Honolulu with a daily continuing service to and from Chicago, Dallas/Fort Worth and New York. The following year American retired the ageing Boeing 707 from its fleet. At the same time it introduced AAdvantage, a revolutionary marketing programme intended to reward frequent fliers; and also the AAirpass, a concept that guarantees

Above: *The 727 proved to be a popular, long-lived aircraft and American bought it in quantity. This 727-23, one of the early versions, was delivered to American in April 1964 and served until 1991 — 27 years!* Peter R. March

fixed personal and business air travel costs for periods ranging between five years to a lifetime.

By the mid-1980s the airline business was even more competitive than ever as low service, cut-rate carriers sprung up in the wake of deregulation. These smaller carriers were in serious danger of taking away the profit from the larger airlines as their bigger aircraft were forced to fly with ever diminishing numbers of passengers and therefore more and more empty seats. Something had to be done to win back passengers' custom and force the opposition into retreat. Thus American in 1985 came up with even larger discount fares — up to 70% reductions became available to the flying public when Ultimate Super Saver fares were introduced. $39 would buy flights of up to 250 miles distance, while $129 was charged for transcontinental flights; all this and at the same time American Airlines' high quality standards of service.

Another effect of deregulation that was felt throughout the 1980s was the emphasis that American put on improving its domestic services, and to this end created a 'hub and spoke' series of connecting airports at convenient locations throughout the entire route system. The chosen premier hubs were Dallas/Fort Worth (which came on-line on 11 June 1981 as American's first hub), Chicago (opened 1982), Miami (opened September 1989), Nashville (opened April 1986), Raleigh/Durham (opened June 1987) and San Juan (opened November 1986). These hubs were also intended to serve as locations where passengers could transfer and connect from one city to another. Furthermore in 1981 American added 11 new cities in Texas, Mississippi, Alabama, Oregon and Florida and seven new routes to its system to strengthen its hub and spoke networks feeding into Dallas/Fort Worth and Chicago. In June a service between Dallas/Fort Worth and Honolulu was started. In the autumn of that

Above: *An American Boeing 727 at St Thomas in March 1988.* Austin J. Brown

Below: *The 767-200 entered service with American in 1982 having been ordered in 1978 to replace the ageing — and gas guzzling — 707s. This is N315AA, a 767-223 which was delivered to American in February 1985.* Peter R. March

year, American brought its planes to Denver, Kansas City and the Yucatan peninsula of Mexico working out from the Dallas/Fort Worth hub.

In April 1982 American introduced an aircraft and passenger interchange service with Alaska Airlines, linking Anchorage and Fairbanks with Houston and Dallas/Fort Worth via Seattle, using Boeing 727 jets. Success followed expansion and on 18 May 1982 American Airlines celebrated its 500-millionth passenger and then welcomed the Boeing 767 to its fleet.

The 19 May 1982 was a red letter day in American history. On that day stockholders voted to approve a plan to reorganise the company so that a new holding company — AMR Corporation — was formed and became the parent company for American Airlines Inc. The intention of the change was to establish increased flexibility in financing and investment for the airline company and its subsidiaries and to bring it to fighting trim in the battle for passengers. Other airlines were also thinking along the same lines and rationalising their operations. Thus in November 1983, American and Pan American World Airways did a swap of aircraft: American exchanged eight Boeing 747s for 15 Pan Am Douglas DC-10s. At the same time, American added the McDonnell Douglas MD-80 to its fleet and called it the 'Super 80'. This was just the start of a massive fleet expansion; on 29 February American placed the largest single aircraft purchase in US aviation history when it ordered 67 Super 80s and placed options on 100 more.

As a further response to deregulation and as a way of working smaller aircraft in and out of otherwise uneconomic locations, American opened its American Eagle system — a network of regional airlines fully integrated into the domestic route system. To help with this new rationalisation, American started construction on new hubs in Nashville, Raleigh/Durham and San Juan.

In spring 1985 American expanded its European service to include a non-stop service between Dallas/Fort Worth–Paris and Dallas/Fort Worth–Frankfurt, and Chicago–Frankfurt. A new Chicago–Honolulu service was started as well.

ROBERT L. CRANDALL

Robert L. Crandall is the current chairman and chief executive officer of AMR Corporation and American Airlines, Inc. After graduating from the University of Rhode Island and receiving a masters degree in business administration from the University of Pennsylvannia, Crandall joined American in 1973 as senior vice president - finance. He worked his way up through the hierarchy at American and in June 1974 he became senior vice president - marketing and has been a member of AMR's board of directors since 1976. He was made president on 16 July 1980. Taking over the position from Albert V. Casey on 1 March 1985, Crandall became chairman and chief executive officer.

Under his chairmanship American developed many innovations such as the Super Saver Fare, American's SABRE automation system, the AAdvantage programme for frequent travellers, the creation of a series of connecting hubs and the development of broadly participative employee relations policies. Such innovations helped to make him *Financial World* magazine's 1991 Silver Award winner in its annual CEO of the year competition, recognising superior business leadership and achievement. In March 1995, the Frontiers of Flight Museum in Dallas bestowed on Crandall its George Haddaway Award for achievement in aviation. He also serves on the board of, amongst others, the World Travel and Tourism Association , the Air Transport Association and the International Air Transport Association.

By 1986 American Airlines had increased in size so much that it employed over 50,000 people for the first time. The following year the company announced that it was getting two new types of long-range wide-bodied jets — 25 A300-600ERs from Airbus Industrie for the Caribbean service, and 15 Boeing 767-300ERs for international routes. 1987 saw American start flying a new international service between Zurich and Geneva, also a non-stop Dallas/Fort Worth-Tokyo service. And for the first time Paris and Frankfurt became destinations from New York.

Until now American Airlines had been largely an east coast and north central United States operation; the west coast was a much under-exploited area. To amend this discrepancy, in July 1987 American Airlines merged with AirCal, a highly successful regional west coast airline, with the intention of gaining a large and immediate presence on the west coast. Furthermore, as the market had changed so much, it made sense for American to

acquire ownership of the Eagle carriers and establish a new subsidiary, AMR Eagle Inc.

In 1988 American Airlines went into the very competitive and highly lucrative second-day door-to-door delivery service: this was such a success that the network was expanded the following year, then again the year after that and in 1988 it became a same-day delivery service. 1988 also saw three new European services introduced on the same day: JFK–Zurich, Dallas/Fort Worth–Madrid and Raleigh/Durham–Paris. This substantially increased American Airlines' European services to which now served a total of nine cities from four US gateways.

With expansion still very much in mind, in 1989 American placed orders for eight McDonnell Douglas MD-11s, a long-range aircraft, with options for an additional 42 planes, plus firm orders for 75 Fokker 100 short-range aircraft with an additional 75 options.

In common with all international airlines, the American fleet had to be modernised

Below: *American runs a substantial number of local feeder services through American Eagle. The four subsidiary companies run a variety of aircraft — but no longer the CASA 212-200 Aviocar seen here.* Austin J. Brown

regularly to make the most of technical developments and safety requirements. Pilot, crew and engineer training is also a crucial cost to be factored in, and to this end American decided to buy the new Boeing 757-200 – the first went into service in 1989. A major consideration in buying this particular aircraft was that the cockpit was similar in configuration to that of the Boeing 767, which considerably reduced staff re-training. Furthermore, the 757 burns a massive average saving of 25% less fuel per seat mile than the Super 80.

In 1989 construction began on American's second major maintenance base at Alliance Airport in Fort Worth. At the same location work also started on Centre PortV, a 750,000sq ft expansion of AMR's corporate headquarters complex. The following year the new, state of the art System Operations Control Center opened at the HQ complex; and American also announced a major expansion of its Tulsa maintenance base.

SABRE

Semi-Automated Business Research Environment

When airline travel became more widely accessible in the 1930s and increasing numbers of people wanted to travel by plane, it rapidly became evident that some form of reservation system was needed to regulate the flow of passengers. Hence American Airlines set their researchers to developing a basic reservations system, this they improved over the next two decades.

Then, in 1953, a chance meeting between Mr C. R. Smith, American's president, and Mr R. Blair Smith a senior sales representative for computer giants IBM on an American Airlines Los Angeles–New York flight took the booking system into the 20th century. In conversation they agreed that a better,

more efficient booking system should be possible given the developments in computer technology just then breaking into mainstream business. They came up with a data processing system which could complete a comprehensive passenger record and which furthermore would make this information available at all points of American's network.

The SABRE system was announced to the world on 5 November 1959. This enabled American for the first time to link a passenger name to a specific seat sold on an airplane. It also made it possible to link passenger inventories with other airlines, leading to the automation of the methods with which airlines handled interline reservations. From this, SABRE has evolved into the world's largest and most sophisticated computerised reservation system, used by corporations and travel agents world-wide to book airline, car and hotel reservations. The facility doesn't stop there: the customer can go on to order flowers, theatre tickets, gifts and other travel-related goods and services.

By 1964 the telecommunications network of the SABRE system extended from coast to coast and from Canada to Mexico. It had become the largest real-time data processing system – second only to the US government's similar system known as SAGE.

In 1975 American Airlines began marketing SABRE to travel agencies throughout the United States and ten years later more than 10,000 travel agency offices used the system to handle their travel reservations.

All this huge amount of data processing equipment needed a safe home and by 1987 American Airlines had completed a $34 million secure underground facility in Tulsa, Oklahoma to house the computer equipment and software. This is the world's largest private real-time computer network and travel information data base, and is designed to be secure against fire, major earthquakes and other disasters.

In 1987 American Airlines offered travel agencies access to SABRE via the personal computer, thus allowing travel professionals to handle word processing, electronic mail and reservation activities from just one terminal. Not long after, this facility was extended to travel agencies in more than 70 countries on six continents. By 1994 more than 27,000 travel agency offices used SABRE on more than 101,000 terminals.

Although already in Latin America, American's presence was not in fact much more than a toe-hold until summer 1990 when, through the acquisition of routes from Eastern Airlines, American obtained the rights to fly to 20 cities in 15 Central and South American countries. To cope with the extra traffic this would bring, American expanded its Miami hub. Now with the expansion bit really between its teeth, the company also introduced a service to Sydney, Australia via Honolulu, Chicago–Glasgow, Miami–Guatemala City, and launched a Los Angeles–Hong Kong service under a code-sharing agreement with Cathay Pacific and Zurich–Budapest under an agreement with MALEV (Hungarian Airlines).

In 1990 to emphasise the company's commitment to cargo, the freight-carrying department of American was restructured as an operating unit and given the name American Airlines Cargo Division. The company proved a success and recorded a steady growth throughout the 1990s. Much of this was thanks to the wholesale introduction of larger passenger aircraft which were capable of carrying more than 50,000lb of cargo in their lower decks. To facilitate all this extra movement in cargo, American tripled the cargo space at their two largest hubs Dallas/Fort Worth and

Chicago, when they built new freight terminals. Handling costs have risen in tandem with wages, so to keep such overheads to a minimum, automation became important and American became the first combination carrier to install the first bar-code-driven tracking and tracing system of freight control. Then in early 1994, all cargo sales representatives were issued with personal notebook computers so they had at their fingertips relevant information on all their freight movements. Through these, operators are given nightly information downloads and full office back-up to provide up to date cargo movement information.

1991 was a particularly busy year for American; in common with its international rivals, American had to provide the greatest in comfort at a competitive price for the international traveller. So in January, American took delivery of its first McDonnell Douglas MD-11, a comfortable 251-seater plane designed for long haul flights such as San Jose-Tokyo. Two months later, on 27 March, American flew its one billionth passenger and in May opened its $26 million, 83,000sq ft western reservations office in Tucson. This same year American introduced the American Flagship Service, a premium three-class transcontinental service between Los Angeles and New York that was designed to allow domestic travellers to experience the comfort and quality of the international service. Then in July American responded to the need for a smaller, more efficient aircraft by taking delivery of the Fokker 100. This 97-seater was specifically bought for intercontinental flights across the USA.

However the biggest and most important breakthrough came in May 1991 when American were able to buy the very profitable but previously unattainable to get, Heathrow operating slots, from TWA . The latter found themselves forced to sell the licence, despite its huge profitability, following their overstretched operations

Above: *A McDonnell Douglas DC-10 taking-off from Los Angeles International. LAX is an important destination for American and a significant hub for American Eagle operations.* Austin J. Brown

which resulted in massive financial problems and bankruptcy crisis. The Heathrow sale was much opposed within the company, but it enabled TWA to survive for a period of bankruptcy protection. This purchase gave American the much sought-after access into the biggest commercial airport in the world and made them the second US carrier to have current representation there.

So, in July 1991 the airline introduced a non-stop service between Heathrow and Boston, New York, Newark, Chicago and Miami. Other services introduced were from Los Angeles–Heathrow, JFK–Gatwick, Chicago–Milan, Miami–Madrid, San Jose–Tokyo with Heathrow routes from TWA. In June 1992 American extended its European growth by starting new services between Chicago–Berlin and Chicago–London Stansted, then in March adding Miami–Paris.

To reduce administration costs and simplify air fares American introduced the Value Pricing Plan. This was a major revision of the pricing structure and an attempt to make fares simple, sensible and fair and to offer customers substantially greater travel flexibility. In essence the new system eliminated fare categories, that in themselves were confusing, and tended to drive high selling costs. However the intense competition from other airlines made the Value Plan unfeasible as they consistently and continuously under-cut American's pricing.

On 16 January 1992, American officially opened the Alliance Maintenance and Engineering Base, at Alliance Airport, (the first industrial airport built in the USA) Fort Worth, Texas. This was the first state-of-the-art airline maintenance facility to be built in the United States in over 20 years.

On 29 April 1993, American inaugurated its first new service from Dallas/Fort Worth in five years, by flying passengers direct to Brussels, the heart of the European Economic Community.

To give their passengers an even greater choice of destinations than the American network allowed and in common practice with their larger competitors, American Airlines set out to achieve code-sharing agreements with smaller, more specialised carriers who could continue passage for customers wanting to get to non-main service destinations. One such agreement was reached in November 1993 when American announced it had reached code sharing agreements with two important carriers, British Midland and Gulf Air. Then, in April 1994, American signed a comprehensive 20-year services agreement with Canadian Airlines International designed to give Canadian access to state-of-the-art airline administrative services and computer technology.

On 26 May 1994 American introduced a service between Gatwick and Nashville and Raleigh/Durham hubs and introduced a regular service from Philadelphia–Heathrow, and upped the frequency between Heathrow and JFK. Then on 16 June a second daily Chicago–Manchester flight gave American a total of 131 non-stop flights a week in the UK–US market; this gave American the right to boast that they flew more services to Britain than any other US airline. By 1994 American Airlines was providing a regular scheduled service to 306 cities across the United States, Mexico, the Caribbean, South and Central America, Asia and Europe. The biggest recent growth areas for American were in Europe and Latin America. By summer 1994 American could claim a total of 250 non-stop operations a week from nine different US gateways to 13 European airports. Furthermore, American served 22 Latin American cities in 16 countries from four US gateways.

In May 1996 American extended its resources further when it announced a code-sharing agreement with Singapore Airlines whereby they offered joint services between Chicago–Singapore via Los

Angeles or San Francisco. In common with practice in much of the United States, since June 1996 American Airlines has not permitted smoking on any American Airlines or American Eagle flights within the United States — this includes flights to and from Hawaii. Until banned on 1 July 1997 smoking was permitted on flights to and from Mexico City, Guadalajara, destinations in Central and South America and flights to Japan.

With competition between airlines at constant fever pitch, any edge over the competition at all is pursued. So when it was announced on 11 June 1996, after weeks of intense speculation and continuous denials, that American Airlines and British Airways jointly planned an alliance which, if sanctioned by their respective governments, would give them control of 60% of flights between the UK and the US, instant uproar broke out. The other airlines immediately denounced such a monopolistic move — the Virgin owner Richard Branson led the opposition by referring to a 'legalised cartel' which would ultimately drive out the smaller operators. The Civil Aviation Authority was also concerned about the inevitable reduction of competition and subsequent increase in fares. However, British Airways' chief executive Bob Ayling and President of American Airlines Don Carty promised the arrangement would bring about a better service because of the competition with other alliances (for example those between Lufthansa, United and SAS (called the Star alliance), the linkup of Delta, Singapore, Swissair and Austrian, and that of Northwest and KLM). At the time this was reported as giving the alliance: 60 percent of Lost Angeles Flights, 71 percent of New York, 94 percent to Chicago, 100 percent to Dallas/Forth Worth; and that ultimately the deal would give British Airways access into the lucrative US domestic market, while American would get the benefit of

Above: *727-223 N862AA was new in 1977.* Austin J. Brown

increased access to Heathrow via BA's 38% hold on all slots.

The merger, originally planned for April 1997, envisaged a co-ordination of passenger and cargo activity, introduction of code-sharing across each other's networks and linking of frequent flying programmes. To facilitate all this, timetables and ticket sales will be pooled. The co-ordination between the companies would be handled by a joint alliance team. All profits from the trans-Atlantic services would be shared by a formula based on percentages. Existing alliances, for example American with Canadian Airlines International, and BA with Qantas, USAir, Deutsche BA and TAT will be unaffected. An indication of the disquiet felt by the other airlines came in December when USAir (now renamed US Airways) announced that, as of 29 March, it would terminate its code-sharing and marketing agreement with BA because of the proposed link-up and sue BA for breach of trust and US competition laws.

The European Union is also unhappy about the proposed merger; it wants to vet the agreement to check that it does not contravene any European stipulations and future plans for an 'Open Skies' agreement in Europe.

In October 1996 a House of Commons Select Committee considered the concentration of the airline industry as inevitable and gave linkup approval, but the agreement was threatened in late August by a government rift and the legal challenge by USAir. Meanwhile across the Atlantic the US government is unhappy about the 'Open Skies' agreement. The alliance has many hurdles to overcome if it is to succeed in its aims, not least the Department of Trade which ruled amongst other things that BA/AA must surrender 168 take-off and landing slots a week at Heathrow if they are to proceed with the alliance. Their report gives the alliance percentages of traffic after linkup as: to Dallas all; Boston 80%; to JFK 86%, LA 45% and Chicago and Miami 81%. With all this opposition from the European Union and the concerned governments, as of July 1997 the agreement had ground to a halt.

To fulfil its ambitions, American placed a huge order with Boeing for 103 airliners worth up to $6.6 billion; at the same time it placed options on a further 527 aircraft to be delivered over the next 20 years. This means that American will buy only Boeing equipment until 2018. This breaks down as 75 next generation B737s powered by CFM56-7s and delivered 1998–2001, 12 777-200s are to be delivered in same time period although a decision has yet to be made on which engine it will use. Another 12 757s and four 767-300ERs will join in 1998–99 and strengthen AA's Pacific routes. Furthermore the purchase rights were settled for 425 next-generation B737s, 38 B777s, 38 B757s and 26 B767-300ERs. These aircraft will replace American's current fleet of B727s, MD-80s and Fokker 100s.

As a stop-gap measure while it arranges for the sale of its MD-11 fleet, American has started to shift Airbus A300s onto its Heathrow–New York route pending arrival of the new 777-200s due for 1998 replacing 767s and MD-11s with A300-600Rs.

In July 1997 with the resolution of its

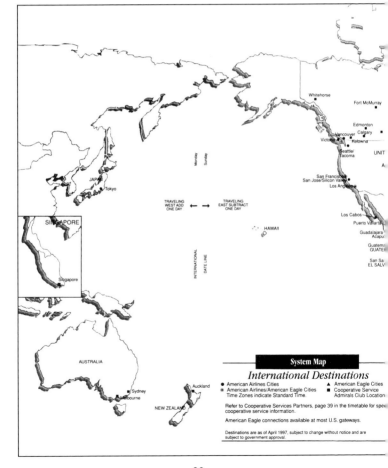

System Map

International Destinations

- ● American Airlines Cities
- ⊛ American Airlines/American Eagle Cities
  Time Zones indicate Standard Time.
- ▲ American Eagle Cities
- ■ Cooperative Service
  Admirals Club Location

Refer to Cooperative Services Partners, page 39 in the timetable for speci cooperative service information.

American Eagle connections available at most U.S. gateways.

Destinations are as of April 1997, subject to change without notice and are subject to government approval.

latest pilots' dispute, American has restructured its huge 103-aircraft fleet replacement programme with Boeing, reaffirming the delivery positions that were lost as a result of the strike. The principal casualty, B737 deliveries, will now run January 1999-2004 and not 1998-2001 as originally planned. American's 12 B757s and four 767-300ERs retain their 1998 delivery dates, although there is some doubt as to whether they will take up the 12 B777-200IGWs or instead opt for the new variants of the 777 — the -200X or -300X.

At the time of going to press, American Airlines still retains its vast Boeing contract, the proposed alliance with British Airways is on a definite hold and the company is lobbying heavily for access to the proposed T5 (Terminal Five) at Heathrow Airport to be able 'to compete on the same playing field as BA'.

Official American Airlines and American Eagle system map showing international destinations.

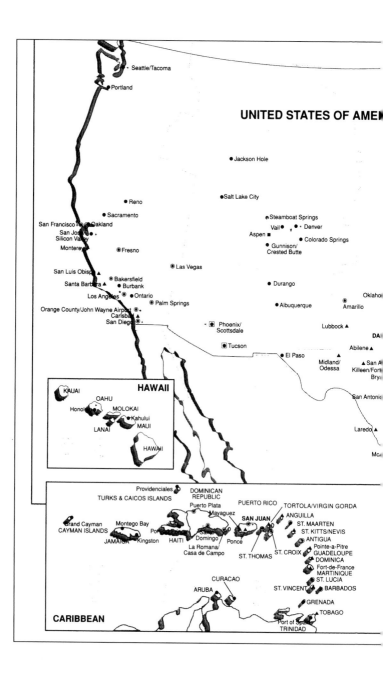

UNITED STATES OF AME...

- Seattle/Tacoma
- Portland

- Jackson Hole

- Salt Lake City

- Reno
- Sacramento
San Francisco Oakland
San Jose
Silicon Valley
Monterey
- Fresno

- Steamboat Springs
Vail - Denver
Aspen
- Colorado Springs
- Gunnison/ Crested Butte

San Luis Obispo
- Bakersfield
Santa Barbara
- Burbank
Los Angeles - Ontario
Orange County/John Wayne Airport
Carlsbad
San Diego

- Las Vegas

- Durango

Oklahom...

- Albuquerque
- Amarillo

- Palm Springs

- Phoenix/ Scottsdale

- Tucson

Lubbock

DA...

Abilene

- El Paso

Midland/ Odessa

San A...
Killeen/Fort
Bry...

San Antonio

Laredo

Mca...

HAWAII

KAUAI
OAHU
Honolu... MOLOKAI
Kahului MAUI
LANAI
HAWAII

CARIBBEAN

Providenciales
TURKS & CAICOS ISLANDS

DOMINICAN REPUBLIC
Puerto Plata
Mayaguez
PUERTO RICO

SAN JUAN
TORTOLA/VIRGIN GORDA
ANGUILLA
ST. MAARTEN

Grand Cayman
CAYMAN ISLANDS
Montego Bay
Po...
JAMAICA Kingston
HAITI
Domingo
La Romana/ Casa de Campo
Ponce
ST. THOMAS
ST. CROIX

ST. KITTS/NEVIS
ANTIGUA
Pointe-a-Pitre
GUADELOUPE
DOMINICA
Fort-de-France MARTINIQUE
ST. LUCIA

CURACAO
ARUBA

ST. VINCENT
BARBADOS

GRENADA
TOBAGO

Port of Spain
TRINIDAD

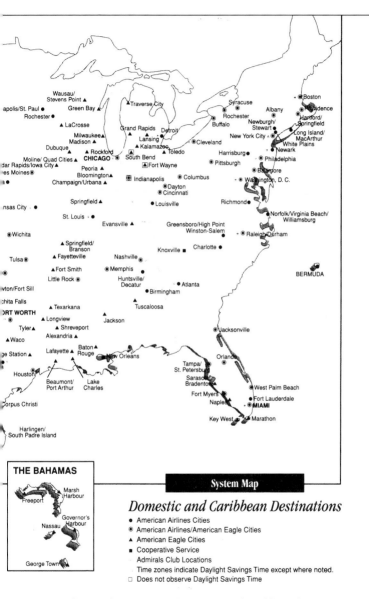

Wausau/
Stevens Point ▲
apolis/St. Paul ●   Green Bay ▲
Rochester ●
▲ LaCrosse
Milwaukee▲
Madison ▲
Dubuque ▲
▲ Rockford
Moline/ Quad Cities ▲   CHICAGO ◉
dar Rapids/Iowa City ▲
es Moines◉   Peoria ▲
Bloomington▲
Champaign/Urbana ▲
a ●

Traverse City▲
Grand Rapids   Detroit
Lansing ●
Kalamazoo ▲
▲ Toledo
South Bend
▲Fort Wayne
◉ Indianapolis
● Columbus
◉Dayton
◉Cincinnati

Syracuse
◉   Albany
Rochester
Buffalo   Newburgh/
New York City ◉   Stewart ●
◉Cleveland

Boston
◉ Providence
Hartford/
● Springfield
Long Island/
MacArthur
White Plains
● Newark

Harrisburg◉
● Pittsburgh

◉ Philadelphia
◉Baltimore
◉ Washington, D. C.

Springfield ▲
St. Louis ●
Evansville ▲
nsas City ●

● Louisville

Greensboro/High Point
Winston-Salem

Richmond●

Norfolk/Virginia Beach/
Williamsburg
◉ Raleigh/Durham

◉ Wichita

▲ Springfield/
Branson
▲ Fayetteville
Tulsa◉
▲Fort Smith
Little Rock ◉

Nashville ◉
Knoxville ■

Charlotte ●

◉ Memphis
Huntsville/
Decatur
● Atlanta
● Birmingham

BERMUDA

vton/Fort Sill
hita Falls
▲ Texarkana
Tuscaloosa
RT WORTH
▲ Longview
Tyler▲   ▲ Shreveport
▲Waco   Alexandria ▲

Jackson

▲
ge Station ▲   Lafayette ▲   Baton▲
Rouge
Houston
Beaumont/
Port Arthur   Lake
Charles
orpus Christi

New Orleans

◉Jacksonville

Tampa/
St. Petersburg
Sarasota/
Bradenton▲

Orlando
◉

●West Palm Beach
Fort Myers◉   ● Fort Lauderdale
Naples●   ◉MIAMI

Key West ●   Marathon

Harlingen/
South Padre Island

THE BAHAMAS

Marsh
Harbour
Freeport
Governor's
Nassau   Harbour

George Town

System Map

Domestic and Caribbean Destinations

● American Airlines Cities
◉ American Airlines/American Eagle Cities
▲ American Eagle Cities
■ Cooperative Service
- Admirals Club Locations
   Time zones indicate Daylight Savings Time except where noted.
□ Does not observe Daylight Savings Time

American Airlines and American Eagle domestic and Caribbean destinations.

Chicago O'Hare International Airport

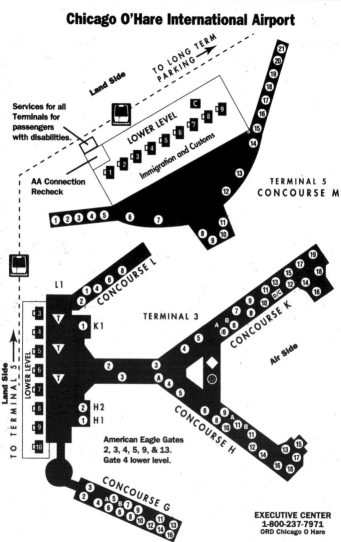

Land Side

TO LONG TERM PARKING

Services for all Terminals for passengers with disabilities.

LOWER LEVEL

Immigration and Customs

C

AA Connection Recheck

TERMINAL 5
CONCOURSE M

CONCOURSE L

L1

TERMINAL 3

CONCOURSE K

Air Side

K1

Land Side

LOWER LEVEL

TO TERMINAL 5

H2

H1

American Eagle Gates
2, 3, 4, 5, 9, & 13.
Gate 4 lower level.

CONCOURSE H

CONCOURSE G

EXECUTIVE CENTER
1-800-237-7971
ORD Chicago O Hare

30

The Hubs

Although American began as a domestic airline, it has today grown into a huge national and international carrier, with services to 306 cities in the US, Mexico, the Caribbean, South and Central America, Asia and Europe. The company's growth in Latin America and Europe has been particularly remarkable. In Europe, the company began its services after the war in 1945, with a trans-Atlantic division called American Overseas Airlines, but after this part of the organisation was sold off in 1950, it was not until 1982 that American re-entered the European market, with a service run between Dallas/Fort Worth and London, Gatwick.

Over the years the company has built up its European routes, with the largest single year of expansion in 1991. At that time, American introduced non-stop services between London, Heathrow and Boston, New York, Newark, Chicago, Los Angeles and Miami; with JFK, New York–London Gatwick, Chicago–Milan, Miami–Madrid and San Jose–Tokyo, also newly connected. This growth continued over the years to include Chicago–Berlin and Miami–Paris (1992), London Gatwick–Nashville and Raleigh/Durham (1994), and a little later London Heathrow–Philadelphia, and increased frequency to JFK, New York. Today American operates more than 130 non-stop flights a week in the US–UK market, and more than 250 non-stop flights from US gateways to European airports.

From a small presence in South America the company has increased its share of the market enormously. Acquiring routes from Eastern Airlines, American obtained the rights to fly to 20 cities in 15 Central and South American countries. The centre of this expansion was American's Miami hub, and today the company serves 22 Latin

Left: *Chicago O'Hare — American's second most important hub.*

Below: *Dallas/Fort Worth handles more than 750 American flights a day.*

Dallas/Fort Worth International Airport
American Eagle Gates 1A-1F lower level, Gates 2A-2C upper level.

American s TRA AM℠, an automated rail service located inside the security area, may be the quickest way to reach the gate for your next flight. The TRAAM runs every two minutes, across from gates 5, 16, 24, and 37.

When you get off the plane and enter the terminal, you will find a gate map and directions to the TRAAM. This map will also tell you whether it is quicker to walk or take the TRAAM to your connecting flight.

Miami International Airport

All American Eagle arrivals are transported to gate E1 lower level.

CONCOURSE E

Land Side

LOWER LEVEL

CONCOURSE D

CONCOURSE C

Air Side

Satellite E Gates E20 through E35 are accessible only by Tram service from main terminal.

Customs located on lower level Concourse E.

Moving walkway for Concourse D is located on level 3.

A connecting walkway is provided between Concourses D and E for the convenience of our passengers. Passengers using this walkway do not

need to clear airport security in order to move between concourses. The walkway is located across from Gate 5 in Concourse D and across from Gate 2 in Concourse E.

All arriving American Eagle passengers are transported to gate E1 lower level.

All departing American Eagle passengers are transported from gate D10A-F lower level directly to their aircraft.

LEGEND

| ▼ TICKETING | 🛄 BAGGAGE | D/C DUTY-FREE CURRENCY EXCHANGE |
| | 😊 ADMIRALS CLUB | ▮▮▮ MOVING WALKWAY |

INFORMATION SUBJECT TO CHANGE. CHECK WITH ANY AMERICAN AIRLINES/AMERICAN EAGLE AGENT FOR FURTHER INFORMATION.

Above: *Miami International Airport — the premier hub between the US and Latin America — is soon to have a new terminal built.*

American cities in 16 countries from four US gateways.

In the domestic market, following deregulation and over a period of years in the 1980s, American built up a series of connecting hubs to provide convenient connections on its entire route system. These hubs were created to serve not only the immediate geographical area but also to link cities to one another, in as versatile and flexible way as possible. They are located in Dallas/Fort Worth, Chicago, Miami and San Juan.

American Airlines largest hub is Dallas/Fort Worth International Airport, its home airport, where more than 750 flights per day to 128 domestic and 17

international destinations are operated. With a new runway, and a new traffic control system now in place, the Dallas/Fort Worth operation continues to grow both in physical size and economic remuneration.

The fierce competition at the second largest hub, Chicago's O'Hare Airport, makes results inevitably smaller. O'Hare is the only airport in the US where two major airlines operate major hubs, the other being United Airlines. While United has more jet slots than American, the company has managed to increase its market share in nine out of ten of the largest markets out of Chicago.

The Miami hub has been increasingly successful both domestically and in its

South American services. Miami is the premier gateway between the US and Latin America, and American plan to sustain this dominance with a new world class terminal soon to begin construction.

At all three of the above hubs the strategy of focussing resources in high volume, business-orientated routes has been working well, with increased market share and profitability the result.

The hub at San Juan, Puerto Rico (while not as large as the others) is also an important part of both American Airlines' and AMR Eagle's network, with 120 flights daily to 37 destinations in the Caribbean and the US.

Right: *San Juan Luis Munoz Marin International Airport sees 120 flights by American daily.*

Hub Profiles

CHICAGO O'HARE INTERNATIONAL

Established	**1982**
Total Investment	$500 million
Principal Traffic Flow	East/West
Number of Gates	48
Daily Departures	344
Non-stop Cities Served	74
International Routes	17
Dedicated Aircraft	165
Airport Employees	11,609

DALLAS/FORT WORTH INTERNATIONAL

Established	1981
Total Investment	$530 million
Principal Traffic Flow	East/West
Number of Gates	58
Daily Departures	520
Non-stop Cities Served	88
International Routes	15
Dedicated Aircraft	256
Airport Employees	15,728

MIAMI INTERNATIONAL

Established	1989
Total Investment	$100 million
Principal Traffic Flow	
US/Europe/Caribbean/Latin America	
Number of Gates	42
Daily Departures	196
Non-stop Cities Served	87
International Routes	44
Dedicated Aircraft	109
Airport Employees	9,071

SAN JUAN LUIS MUNOZ MARIN INTERNATIONAL

Established	1986
Total Investment	$308million
Principal Traffic Flow	US/Caribbean
Number of Gates	16
Daily Departures	52
Non-stop Cities Served	21
International Routes	7
Dedicated Aircraft	25
Airport Employees	2,593

Affiliated Companies

American Eagle

When the airline business in the USA was deregulated in 1978, a number of smaller communities lost their major airline service, or where the service wasn't lost completely, the number of flights was severely reduced. Many cities lost their choice of flights to outbound destinations, and even reduced to only one. To fill this void a number of small operators appeared, providing the service between the outlying communities and the big cities. However they could not afford to compete with the large airlines in terms of service and comfort. So, reasoned American Airlines, there was a obvious need for regional carriers who would serve the smaller communities with big airline levels of service and sophistication.

Thus American Airlines gave birth to American Eagle in November 1984 to serve and support these smaller but nonetheless vital passenger and freight requirements of the outlying communities. In essence this was a network of regional airlines fully integrated into the American Airlines domestic route system. It operates a vast local feeder service operated by four subsidiaries under the American Eagle banner. These provided more than 1,800 flights daily by 1996. Here they offered something not available previously: frequent flights between American Airlines hubs and the smaller communities all with a high level of passenger service. Their aim was 'seamless' service, so a passenger connecting through American Airlines services would only notice that the size of the plane had changed and nothing else – the level and quality of service would be the same on American Airlines and American Eagle.

The venture has proved popular and successful and passenger usage has grown accordingly. The service started with just 60 flights a day to nine cities from Dallas/Fort Worth until by 1994 Eagle has more than 1,700 flights a day to more than 170 cities large and small, including eight hubs in the United States, Canada, the Bahamas and the Caribbean with a modern fleet of turboprop aircraft. American Eagle also offers many of the same services as American Airlines — like pre-reserved seating, advanced booking passes and mileage credit.

As this side of airline passenger business got more successful, the nature of the system itself had to change. Originally a network of nine independent carriers, they became four airlines all owned by AMR Eagle, Inc, a wholly-owned subsidiary of AMR Corporation, the parent of American Airlines.

Executive Airlines headquarters at San Juan, Puerto Rico. An American Eagle carrier since 15 June 1986, became an AMR Eagle subsidiary on 7 December 1989. Flies San Juan, Puerto Rico–Caribbean, and Miami and other Florida locations to the Bahamas.
Aircraft: 8 ATR-42, 3 ATR-72, 11 Shorts 360. Total of 22 aircraft.

Flagship Airlines headquarters at Nashville, Tennessee. Operates out of Nashville, Miami, New York and Raleigh/Durham. Nashville Eagle which served Nashville and later RDU hubs, was the first owned carrier in 1987. Command Airways operated out of New York/JFK and was purchased in 1990 by AMR Eagle. In 1991 Command and Nashville were combined into a new carrier called Flagship Airlines.
Aircraft: 46 SAAB 340B, 11 ATR-42. Total of 57 aircraft.

Simmons Airlines headquarters at Fort Worth, Texas. Founded in 1978, joined the American Eagle system on 1 October 1985 and became an AMR subsidiary on 8 August 1988. Its main bases are at Chicago, Dallas/Fort Worth. Simmons bought the assets of Metroflight Airlines at DFW, the last independent carrier, out of bankruptcy in late 1992.

Aircraft: 8 SAAB 340B, 25 SAAB 340B *Plus*, 27 ATR-42, 30 ATR-72. Total of 88 aircraft.

Wings West Airlines headquarters at San Luis Obispo, California. Founded in 1981, American Eagle carrier since 1 June 1986. Purchased by the AMR Corporation on 9 August 1988. It provides a network of services based on hubs at Los Angeles and Dallas/Fort Worth.

Aircraft: 3 Jetstream 32, 40 SAAB 340B. Total of 43 aircraft.

American Eagle Hub Profiles

CHICAGO O'HARE INTERNATIONAL

Established	1987
Number of Gates	5
Daily departures	148
Non-stop cities served	26
International routes	0
Dedicated aircraft	39
Airport employees	1,075

DALLAS/FORT WORTH

Established	1984
Number of Gates	8
Daily departures	267
Non-stop cities served	34
International routes	0
Dedicated aircraft	39
Airport employees	2,100

LOS ANGELES INTERNATIONAL

Established	1986
Number of Gates	2
Daily departures	102
Non-stop cities served	12
International routes	0
Dedicated aircraft	15
Airport employees	500

MIAMI INTERNATIONAL

Established	1989
Number of Boarding areas	5
Daily departures	83
Non-stop cities served	15
International routes	5
Dedicated aircraft	22
Airport employees	943

NEW YORK JFK INTERNATIONAL

Established	1986
Number of Gates	4
Daily departures	76
Non-stop cities served	17
International routes	2
Dedicated aircraft	27
Airport employees	640

SAN JUAN LUIS MUÑOZ MARIN INTERNATIONAL

Established	1986
Number of Gates	2
Daily departures	73
Non-stop cities served	18
International routes	15
Dedicated aircraft	22
Airport employees	700

American Airlines Cargo

American Airlines Cargo is one of the largest scheduled air freight carriers in the world, providing a full range of freight and mail services to shippers throughout the system. Shipments can be made to virtually every corner of the globe, if not through American Cargo direct, then through their network of co-operative agreements reached with other companies.

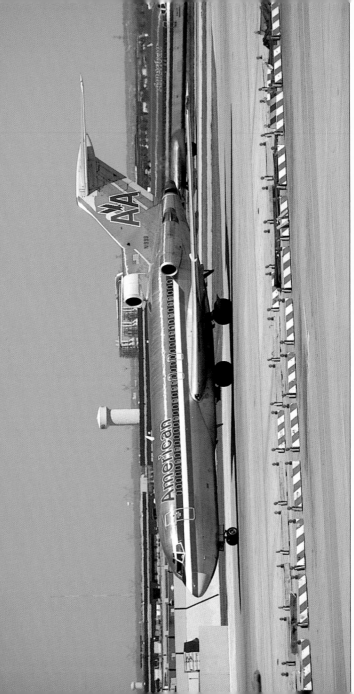

Above: N1998, a 727-23, was delivered in November 1965 and served with American until 1993. Leo Marriott

Above: N441AA — an MD-82 — was delivered to American in September 1987, one of over 200 examples bought by the company. Leo Marriott

Domestic services include: a priority parcels service; Allocated Space express AAir – a service for cargo contract holders which makes freight available two hours after arrival at the terminal; standardAAir, a second day delivery service.

International services include: On Board Courier, a flight specific, dimension and weight controlled carrier service which must be accompanied by a courier; Priority Parcels Service, again flight and dimensions specific; expressAAir - Allocated Space, flight specific for contract customers, containerised freight available three hours after flight arrival, and bulk freight available four hours after arrival; expressAAir, same but for non-contract customers; standardAAir, freight available 72 hours after midnight.

In addition there are some specialised services:

Garment-on-Hanger Shipments, this speeds clothing shipments from the factory to showroom floors; Jim Wilson Service, a shipment facility for the deceased; Live Animal Transportation, anything from show dogs to exotic wildlife; Perishable shipments, speedy handling for fruit and vegetables, seafood, flowers and other perishables.

American Airlines Cargo Division Agreements

Japan Airlines AA Cargo acts as a general sales agent in 14 states in the US and 26 countries in the Caribbean and Latin America. In return Japan Air acts as general sales agent for AA Cargo in Japan, Thailand, and other south-west Asian countries.

Alitalia Cargo AA Cargo acts as general sales agents for Alitalia in most Latin American countries, the Caribbean and parts of Canada. Alitalia acts as general sales agents for AA Cargo in Italy, parts of Africa and the eastern Mediterranean.

Canadian Airlines AA Cargo acts for Canadian throughout the United States, Latin America and the Caribbean. In return Canadian acts as general sales agent for AA Cargo throughout Canada.

Co-Operative Service Partners

To make international travel as seamless as possible for its passengers, American Airlines has developed co-operative service relationships (sometimes called code sharing) with other selected airlines around the world. These give American customers easy access to destinations not served directly by American They have developed a fully integrated system with these partners, so one ticket will see a passenger through on however many airlines it takes to get to their destination. Pre-reserved seats, advanced booking passes and reliable baggage transfers are all part of the service.

Partners are:

Aspen Mountain Air	Dallas/Fort Worth–Aspen. Aspen–Denver
British Midland Since November 1993	From the US — Amsterdam, Belfast, Edinburgh, Frankfurt, Glasgow, Leeds/Bradford, Teesside, Zurich (via Heathrow)
Canadian Since June 1995	From the US — Canada and cities within Canada

Gulf Air Since Febrary 1994	From the US — Abu Dhabi, UAE, Bahrain, Doha, Qatar and Muscat, Oman (via Heathrow)
Lone Star Airlines	Dallas/Fort Worth–Knoxville, Tennessee
LOT (Polish Airlines) Since July 1996	From Chicago, New York JFK — Warsaw
Qantas Since November 1994	From the US — Sydney, Melbourne, Auckland (all via Los Angeles)
Singapore Airlines Since July 1996	Chicago–Singapore (via Los Angeles or San Francisco)
SAA (South African Airlines) Since November 1992	From the US — Johannesburg (via New York JFK), Cape Town, Johannesburg (via Miami)

Other agreements are under negotiation: these are with China Airlines, El Al Israel Airlines, TACA Group, BWIA , and Transaero Airlines.

Below: *Currently American has no Boeing 747s, the timetabled services using the aircraft being operated by Qantas Airways, South African Airways or Canadian Airlines International. This is N601AA a 747SP31 which served with American from July 1986 until 1993.* Leo Marriott

Above: *DC-10-10 N152AA at Coolidge Field, Antigua.* Austin J. Brown

AMERICAN AIRLINES AIRCRAFT

Above: *All of American's DC-10-30s were bought second-hand in the early 1980s. Here is N137AA which was bought from Air New Zealand.* Austin J. Brown

McDonnell Douglas DC-10

	DC-10-10	DC-10-30
First flight	29 August 1970	
Wingspan	155ft 4in (47.34m)	165ft4in (50.39m)
Wing Area	3,550sq ft (329.8sq m)	3,647sq ft (338.8sq m)
Length	182ft 3in (55.3m)	180ft 8in (55.06m)
Height	58ft 1in (17.7m)	58ft 1in (17.7m)
Seating	3 crew, 237-290 passengers	3 crew, 273 passengers
Cargo volume	3,180cu ft (89cu m)	3,655cu ft (103.5cu m)
Fuel capacity	145,200lb (65,921kg)	245,566lb (111,420kg)
Weight empty	248,100lb (112,637kg)	267,197lb (121,198kg)
Max take off weight	430,000lb (195,200kg)	580,000lb (263,085kg)
Max range max fuel	3,800nm (7,040km)	6,505nm (12,055km)
Max range max payload	2,000nm (3,700km)	4,005nm (7,415km)
Cruising speed	464kt (860kph)	490kt (908kph)
Powerplant	3 x General Electric (GE) CF6-6D 40,000lb (178kN) or D1 41,000lb (182,4kN) thrust turbofans	3 x GE CF6-50C 51,000lb (226.9kN) thrust turbofans
Service ceiling	42,000ft (12,810m)	42,000ft (12,810m)

First delivery to AA	N103AA on 29 July 1971	Second-hand purchase
Number bought by AA	53 [1]	8 [2]
Number in service end 1996	16 [3]	5 [4]

[1] *New* — 5 in 1971, 20 in 1972, 3 in 1978, 4 in 1979, 3 in 1980, 1 in 1981.
Second-hand — 3 in 1983, 8 in 1984, 2 in 1985, 2 in 1986, 2 in 1987.
[2] *Second hand* — 1 in 1981, 4 in 1984, 2 in 1985, 1 in 1986.
[3] Also 10 on lease to Hawaiian and 13 in store. See fleetlist.
[4] Also 3 on lease to Transaero. See fleetlist.

The DC-10 was born out of the US Air Force's CX-HLS heavy-lift cargo requirement, which led to competitive studies from Boeing (whose submission helped considerably the development of the 747), Lockheed (the eventual winner with the C-5 Galaxy) and Douglas. In the aftermath of the loss of this order there was an attempt to produce a civil version — a 650-seat, double-deck, wide-bodied aircraft which was just too big for the time. At this juncture American circulated to the same big three companies — Boeing, Lockheed and Douglas — a specification for the size of aircraft it required to increase its passenger carrying abilities without increasing air movements. American proposed an aircraft that should be able to carry 250 passengers in wide-bodied comfort over ranges of 1,000–2,000 miles depending on the length of the runways used — so the longer range would cover West Coast–Chicago routes where there was no limit to runway length and the lower range would be applicable when shorter runways were used, specifically at New York's LaGuardia airport where the aircraft had also to be small enough to fit the terminals. Merger with McDonnell on 28 April 1967 eased Douglas's financial

Below: *DC-10-10 N154AA takes-off from Chicago O'Hare, June 1989. N154AA started life in late 1972 with National Airlines. It entered American service in 1983 and was withdrawn in 1995.* Austin J. Brown

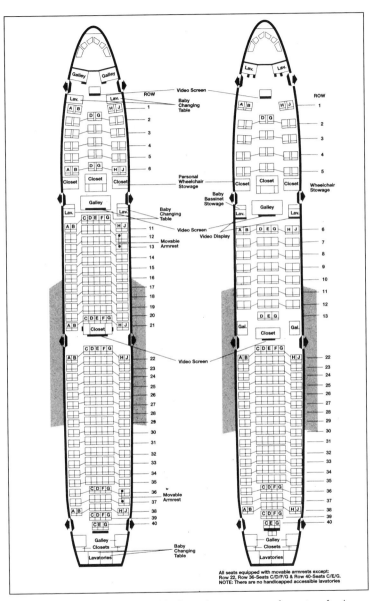

Above: American's pocket timetable shows these seating configurations for the DC-10: left Hawaii and special markets, right transcontinental.

43

Above: *An excellent overview of DC-10-10 N135AA showing well the tail engine and empennage.* Peter R. March

problems and the DC-10 became the first McDonnell Douglas aircaft and the last to carry the famous 'DC' branding. McDonnell Douglas's capital, and a new project manager, saw the response to American's proposal refined down to its final form — a trijet, the third engine being necessary to give the additional power needed to use shorter runways. In the light of the CX-HLS result, it was perhaps only just that the DC-10 should beat the Lockheed proposal (another trijet, the TriStar) for the order and on 19 February 1968 American signed a contract for 50 DC-10s — 25 on firm order, with 25 options. The prototype DC-10 (N103AA which would eventually be the first aircraft delivered to American) was painted in American colours during flight testing. The first aircraft were handed over to American and United (who had ordered 60) in a joint ceremony at Long Beach on 29 July 1971. Both companies raced to be first to get the DC-10 into service and, as befitted its role in the aircraft's development, American was first on 5 August 1971 when it inaugurated services on its Los Angeles-Chicago route with the first DC-10 'Luxury Liner', N103AA. It used a 34 first class/174 coach class seating arrangement. By the end of December 1972 American had received all 25 of its

initial order, the last 10 aircraft having additional fuel tanks to allow use on longer sectors such as Chicago-Honolulu. The DC-10-30, an intercontinental version with uprated engines was rolled-out on 1 June 1972 and the first flight took place three weeks later. It would enter commercial service with Swissair on 15 December 1972. A series of mishaps to the DC-10 were to give it a probably unwarranted bad reputation. The first was on 12 June 1972 when N103AA left Detroit for Buffalo and New York. At 12,000ft what seemed like explosive decompression took place and the pilot had to make an emergency landing. Later investigations discovered that the rear cargo door had come adrift. The resulting McDonnell Douglas recommen-dations were not able to stop a similar problem killing all 346 passengers and crew of a Turkish Airlines DC-10-10. Then the spectacular crash of American's N110AA at Chicago on 25 May 1979 led to a five-week grounding of all DC-10s. The crash saw 13 crew, 259 passengers and two people on the ground killed as the aircraft crashed on take-off from Chicago O'Hare to Los Angeles. The reason was a broken bolt in the engine mounting and further cracks in the aft pylon bulkheads which were found on inspection. It took 37 days before

Above: *Replaced by the MD-11 on McDonnell Douglas's construction line, the DC-10 has proved an excellent workhorse despite its early problems.* Austin J. Brown

permission came from the FAA for the DC-10 to resume flying. The disasters did not stop American taking new DC-10s. A further 15 aircraft (11 -10s, 4 -30s, Pan Am aircraft inherited from National) were bought as were 10 new examples (of the original 25 options) between 1978 and 1980. A further three ex-Air New Zealand and one ex-KLM DC-10-30s brought the fleet up to 53 in 1985. Second-hand -30s arrived as transatlantic sectors were added, but American started to withdraw -10s from service in June 1993. Some were broken up, others sold to Federal Express and by the end of 1996 only 12 -10s and five -30s were still in service (although others were out on lease or in store). American is planning to retain its DC-10 fleet but will modify and update them with some of the MD-11 features. The DC-10s are used on long-distance transcontinental flights of around 2,000 miles — for example, New York JFK–Los Angeles is 2,475 miles — although its regular services to Honolulu from Chicago and Dallas/Fort Worth are much longer, 4,243 and 3,784 miles respectively. Seating on these flights is 34 first class and 256 coach class as against the 28 first, 52 business and 157 coach class of the transcontinental services.

McDonnell Douglas MD-80

	MD-82	MD-83
First flight	8 January 1981	17 December 1984
Wingspan	107ft 10in (32.87m)	1o7ft 10in (32.87m)
Wing area	1,029sq ft (112.3sq m)	1,029sq ft (112.3sq m)
Length	147ft 11in (45.08m)	147ft 11in (45.08m)
Height	29ft 7in (9.02m)	29ft 7in (9.02m)
Seating	2 crew, 139 passengers	2 crew, 139 passengers
Cargo volume	1,243cu ft (35.2cu m)	1,243cu ft (35.2cu m)
Fuel capacity	39,100lb (17,751kg)	39,100lb (17,751kg)
Weight empty	82,300lb (37,364kg)	80,230lb (136620kg)
Max take-off weight	149,500lb (67,812kg)	160,000lb (72,580kg)
Max range max payload	2,140 (3,445km)	2,725 (4,387km)
Cruising speed	510kt (944kph)	575 (925kph)
Powerplant	2 x Pratt & Whitney (P&W) JT8D-217A/B 20,000lb (88.97kN) thrust turbofans	2 x P&W JT8D-219 21,000lb (93.42kN) thrust turbofans
Service ceiling	37,000ft (11,285m)	37,000ft (11,285m)
First delivery to AA	12 May 1983	3 June 1987
Number bought by AA	228	32
Number in service end 1996	228	32

The twin-jet DC-9 family, which includes what is now known as the MD-80 and MD-90, is one of the world's most popular. Over 2,000 aircraft — 976 of them DC-9s — were built from the early 1960s onwards. Surprisingly, considering its interest in the MD-80, American did not buy the DC-9 at all, but its 260-strong fleet of MD-80s has been a major factor in the type's continued success. The DC-9 was produced as a smaller, short/medium range, companion to the long-range DC-8, Douglas's first jet airliner, which was a contemporary of — and competitor to — the Boeing 707. 556 DC-8s were built between 1958 and 1972, a figure which reflects the success of the 707 because the 'Super 60' series, especially re-engined as Srs 70s, was a very good aircraft indeed. Douglas discussed the design of the DC-9 with a number of airlines, first order and launch order coming from Delta in May 1963. As with the DC-8, the DC-9's main

competitor was a Boeing aircraft — in this case the 737, which had the advantages of a wider body allowing six-abreast seating and more freight capacity. It had the disadvantage of reaching the market three years after the DC-9; indeed, on the day the 737 flew first (9 April 1967) the 100th DC-9 was delivered. The success of the DC-9 was not just based on its timing. It proved to be a perfect platform for modification and stretching — as is evidenced by its family's continued construction into the later 1990s. The DC-9-50 saw a stretch to 125ft 7in allowing a maximum of 139 passengers; the Super 80 series came along at 147ft 10in and a maximum of 172 passengers. With the Super 80 series, from June 83, came a new name to emphasise the 'McDonnell' Douglas development rather than the Douglas ancestry. The first of the MD-80 series, the MD-81, was quickly upengined into the MD-82, which was announced on

16 April 1979 and made its first flight on 8 January 1981. Regarded as being particularly suitable for operation from hot and high airports, the -82 was certificated on 30 July 1981 and entered service with Republic Airways in August 1981. From autumn 1982 it was offered with a higher gross weight option and improved engines. American's first order for 20 MD-82s was placed in September 1982. The first American MD-82, N218AA, was delivered on 4 May 1983; the first order for 20 was filled by the end of the year. So pleased was the airline with what it received that in 1984 it put in a massive order for 167 aircraft (67 firm with options on a further 100), revitalising sales of the MD-80 with the largest single order by any airline in the US at that time. On 31 January 1983 McDonnell Douglas announced the MD-83, which differed principally in having higher thrust turbofans, an improved max take-off weight and more fuel capacity. It flew first on 17 December 1984 and entered service in September of that year with Finnair. American took possession of the first of 25 MD-83s on 3 June 1987; a further seven MD-82s would be converted to MD-83 standard in early 1993. In American service the MD-80s are configured for 12 first class and 130 coach class passengers. Their main task is the medium-range sector, their longest flight being from the West Coast cities to Chicago — for example San Jose, California-Chicago is 1,829 miles; San Fransisco-Chicago is 1,846. Their shortest scheduled flight is probably the 246 miles from Dallas Fort Worth to San Antonio. Consideration is being given to re-engining the MD-80s or taking the MD-90.

Below: *MD-82 N7548A has been in service with American since 1991. The photograph shows clearly the disparity in size between the two aircraft types — the DC-10 is nearly 30ft higher and 35ft longer.* Peter R. March

Above: American was so pleased with the MD-82 that it ordered 67 with 100 options following receipt of its initial models. This MD-82, N497AA was delivered in 1989. Peter R. March

Above: *The Boeing 767-223ER first flew in 1984 and entered American service in 1985. N338AA arrived in late 1987.* Peter R. March

Boeing 767

	767-223	767-223ER	767-323ER
First flight	26 September 1981	6 March 1984	19 December 1986
Wingspan	156ft 1in (47.57m)	156ft 1in (47.57m)	156ft 4in/47.64m
Wing area	3,050sq ft (283.2sq m)	3,050sq ft (283.2sq m)	3,050sq ft/283.2sq m
Length	159ft 2in (48.51m)	159ft 2in (48.51m)	180ft 3in/54.94m
Height	52ft (15.85m)	52ft (15.85m)a	52ft/15.85m
Seating (usual)	2/3 crew, 172 passengers	2/3 crew, 166 passengers	2+202
Cargo volume	3,070cu ft (87cu m)	3,070cu ft (87cu m)	4,030cu ft/114.1cu m
Fuel capacity	112,309lb (50,988kg)	137,527lb (62,437kg)	161,738lb/73,429kg
Weight empty	163900lb (74,344lb)	168,600lb (76,476kg)	205,600lb/93,342kg
Max take-off weight	315,000lb (142,881kg)	387,000lb (175,540kg)	400,000lb/181,600kg
Range	3,850nm (7,135km)	6,805nm (12,611km)	5,760nm/10,674km
Cruising speed	493kt (914kph)	493kt (914kph)	486kt/900kph
Powerplant	2 x GE CF6-80C2B2 52,500lb (233.5kN)thrust turbofans	2 x GE CF6-80C24B 57,900lb (257.7kN) thrust turbofans	2 x GE CF6-80C2B6 61,500lb/ 273.6kN thrust turbofans
Service ceiling	40,000ft (12,192m)	40,000ft (12,192m)	42,000ft/12,810m
First delivery to AA	4 November 1982	18 November 1985	19 February 1988
Number bought by AA	10 [1]	20 [2]	41 [3]
Number in service end 1996	8	22	41 [4]

[1] 3 in 1982, 5 in 1983, 2 in 1984.
[2] 5 in 1985, 7 in 1986, 7 in 1987, 1 in 1988.
[3] 15 in 1988, 3 in 1991, 10 in 1992, 6 in 1993, 3in 1994 and 4 in 1995.
[4] on order for delivery 1998.

The Boeing 767 project first saw light of day when Boeing released drawings of a 200-passenger, four-engined (two underwing, two on rear fuselage) aircraft in August 1971. As is always the case with a new jet aircraft, development time is considerable — they are too expensive to rush! — and the upturn of 737 sales meant that Boeing was in no hurry to produce an in-house competitor. It was, therefore, only in February 1978 that Boeing announced its future 757, 767 and 777 projects. The 767-100 was an all-new wide-bodied aircraft which had been designed to fit an American requirement to carry 175 passengers in a seven-abreast configuration over a range of 2,000nm; the 767-200 had extra seating and was based on a United requirement for 190 passengers to be carried. It was the latter that, following more design changes, became the final 767 as United became launch customer on 14 July 1978 with an order for 30 planned for mid-1982 entry into service. American interest had centred on the then 777 project — a trijet version of the 767 with both transcontinental and oceanic versions. When that was shelved, American looked again at the 767 and, on 15 November 1980, announced a firm order for 30 767s with options for a further 20, all powered with GE CF6-80A 48,000lb (213.5kN) thrust engines — the first 767s capable of non-stop transcontinental operations. The firm orders were for delivery over a 28-month period starting in October 1982; options covered delivery positions in 1983–86. The unit price of a 767 at that time was $25 million — which shows how inflation hit prices; today's costing for a 767-200 is $77–87 million. The first 767 flew on 26 September 1981 and the type entered service the next year. In American service the 767 was designated 767-223; the company received its first aircraft, N301AA, on 4 November 1982. It entered service on the 21st of the same month on the San Fransisco–New York transcontinental route, seating 24 First Class and 180 economy class passengers. The longer-range -200ER version — with an extra wing section fuel tank allowing — first flew on 6 March 1984, entering service in May 1984. The first of 20 American -223ERs arrived in February 1985. Boeing stretched the 767 with the 767-300 which flew first on 30 January 1986. The 21ft 1in (6.42m) stretch saw two sections added to the fuselage in front of and behind the wing. At the end of 1986 the extended range version of the 767-300 flew for the first time: American was launch customer for this version, ordering 15. It was designated 767-323ER, powered by CF6-80C2 engines and had 215 seats for American's new European services. Deliveries commenced early in 1988 and further orders took the fleet to 41, the last aircraft, N391AA, being delivered on 16 February 1995. At the end of 1996, American had four more -323ERs on order for delivery in 1998. The economic use of

Above: *767-223ER N313AA retracts its undercarriage and climbs steadily after take-off..* Austin J. Brown

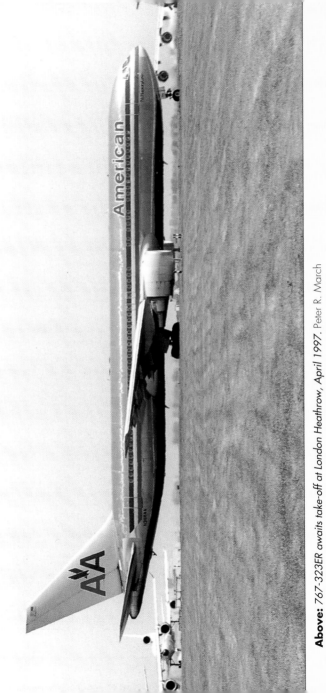

Above: *767-323ER awaits take-off at London Heathrow, April 1997.* Peter R. March

Above: *Boeing 767-323ER N39364, was delivered in 1988.* Peter R. March

reliable, extended-range twin-jets over transoceanic — especially transatlantic — routes allowed a change to the established operating rules. ETOPS (Extended range Twin-jet Operations) is a highly significant modification to the long-established US FAA 1953 dictat, which said that twin-engined aircraft must always be within an hour of an airfield at zero wind speed and normal cruising speed — this usually worked out to be 400nm (841km). While it was possible — as TWA showed by inaugurating the first 767 non-stop transcontinental flights — to fly these distances, the 60min rule reduced the economic use of twin-jets over the Atlantic. The cost of fuel and, more importantly, the substantial improvement in engine reliability since the original 1953 pronouncement led to an extension of the length of time twin-engined aircraft can operate over oceans to 120 minutes, assuming the engine/aircraft combination gets certified. (The acronym ETOPS became EROPS — extended range operations — in 1989.) American was among the pioneers of ETOPS services, commencing 767 flights to Switzerland from Chicago on 1 April 1986, followed by Dallas–Frankfurt and Dallas–London services using -223ERs. Today American's 767s are used on medium-range transcontinental flights — such as the 2,475-mile (3,982km) New York JFK–Los Angeles service, or that from Seattle to Miami, which is a flight of 2,724 miles (4,383km). However, they are predominantly used on long-range services, with daily -223ER or -323ER flights to a variety of destinations in Europe, such as London Heathrow (from New York JFK, Chicago, Miami, Los Angeles and Boston); Paris Orly (from Chicago, Dallas/Fort Worth, Miami, Boston, New York JFK); Madrid (from Miami); and Frankfurt (from Chicago and Dallas/Fort Worth). South America is also served by 767s — for example flights to Sao Paulo, Brazil by -323ER (a distance of 5,111 miles/8,224km). Many of American's scheduled 767 flights are over 4,500 miles (7,240km) in distance with Dallas/Fort Worth–Frankfurt being 5,143 miles (8,275km), Los Angeles–London Heathrow 5,456miles (8,780km) and New York JFK–Buenos Aires, Argentina 5,281 miles (8,497km). In American service the three 767 seating configurations, as outlined in the company's excellent pocket timetable, are: 767-200 Domestic operations — 14 first class, 30 business and 128 coach class; 767-200 International operations — 10 first class, 30 business and 126 economy class. 767-300 International operations — 15 first class, 30 business and 157 coach class.

54

A✠A

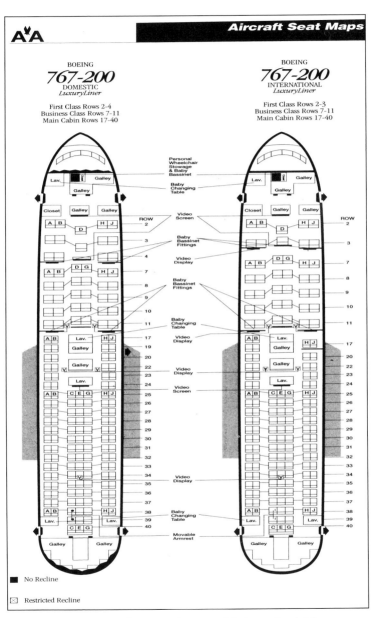

BOEING
767-200
DOMESTIC
LuxuryLiner

First Class Rows 2-4
Business Class Rows 7-11
Main Cabin Rows 17-40

BOEING
767-200
INTERNATIONAL
LuxuryLiner

First Class Rows 2-3
Business Class Rows 7-11
Main Cabin Rows 17-40

Personal
Wheelchair
Stowage
& Baby
Bassinet

Baby
Changing
Table

Video
Screen

Baby
Bassinet
Fittings

Video
Display

Baby
Bassinet
Fittings

Baby
Changing
Table

Video
Display

Video
Display

Video
Screen

Video
Display

Baby
Changing
Table

Movable
Armrest

■ No Recline

☒ Restricted Recline

Above: *767-200 seating layouts — domestic at left, international right.*

55

Above: *New at the end of 1990, 757-223 N634AA is one of 90 757s currently in service with American. 12 more are on order.* Peter R. March

Boeing 757-223

First flight:	19 February 1982
Wingspan:	124ft 10in (38.05m)
Wing area:	1,994sq ft (185.25sq m)
Length:	155ft 3in (47.32m)
Height:	44ft 6in (13.56m)
Seating:	2 crew, 188 passengers
Cargo volume:	1,790cu ft (50.7cu m)
Fuel capacity:	75,500lb (34,277kg)
Weight empty:	129,100lb (58,611kg)
Max take-off weight:	240,000lb (108,960kg)
Range:	3,700nm (6,857km)
Cruising speed:	460kt (850kph)
Powerplant:	2 x Rolls-Royce RB211-535E4B 42,540lb (188.8kN) thrust turbofans
Service ceiling:	42,000ft (12,810m)

First delivery to AA: 17 July 1989
Number bought by AA: 90 (8 in 89, 19 in 90, 23 in 91, 19 in 92, 6 in 93, 6 in 94, and 9 in 95)
Number in service end 1996: 90 (12 on order for delivery 1998–99)

With the 727 getting long in the tooth, Boeing had been looking for a suitable replacement. The first thought was simply to stretch the reliable and best-selling trijet 727 itself. Indeed, this is what was shown in 1974 and at the Paris Air Show in 1975. United had shown interest in this 727-300B, a stretch that would increase passenger numbers to 189 and the improved engines would take the range out to 2,300 miles (3,700km), but no airline would put in a confirmed order because of the need for quieter and more fuel efficient engines — a particular issue in the oil crisis of the 1970s. Boeing therefore changed tack and, after a variety of design changes, in February 1978 reached a formula, now christened 757, that proved successful enough to gain orders. It used the 727's fuselage cross-section, a new flightdeck, a modified empennage and a totally new wing. It was designed to carry 150–170 passengers, and would have a pair of fuel-efficient, quiet turbofans. This 757 was launched in March 1979: British Airways and Eastern were launch customers. To save costs there was commonality of systems with the 767, especially in the flightdeck and avionics equipment — so much so that pilots

Above: *Overhead view of 757-223 N654A in delivery month, October 1991.*
Peter R. March

could be cleared to fly both 757 and 767 without conversion. The 757 was produced in parallel with the 767 — the latter actually the first to fly despite the numerical sequence. The 757 took to the air on 19 February 1982 and received certification on 17 December 1982 (FAA) and in January 1983 (CAA). Entering service in January 1983 with Eastern, the early 757-200s were the first Boeing aircraft launched with non-American powerplants, being powered by Rolls-Royce RB211-535Cs (this was no coincidence considering BA was one of the launch customers). First flight of a US (Pratt & Whitney) -engined version was on 14 March 1984. The passenger accommodation was usually 16 first class and 187 economy giving a total of 203. The 757-200 was one of the first aircraft to have electronic displays, with many routine tasks automated. It quickly established itself on the world market, and has gone through little developmental change since. In 1985 the 757-200ER was certified for ETOPS with Rolls-Royce engines, followed by Pratt & Whitney-powered versions in 1990. (See 767 section for explanation of the acronym ETOPS, now known as EROPS.) American

originally looked at 757 purchase in January 1981 when it was reported to have ordered 15 757s with P&W engines with a further 15 options — an order worth $375 million. Instead it bought DC-9-82s and it would not be until 25 May 1988 that the airline bought 50 RB211-535E4-powered aircraft with 50 options. Delivery was set for 1989-93 and they would replace 727s and 737s, the low noise of the Rolls-Royce engines being critical. Another 16 757-200s were ordered in mid-1991. On 31 March 1992 orders/deliveries stood at 91/56 with the first, N611AM, having been delivered on 17 July 1989. Seating arrangements on the American 757s is 22 in first class, with 166 in the main cabin. It is used on medium-range routes, varying from short hops like Dallas/Fort Worth to Colorado Springs (592 miles/953km) or Denver (644 miles/1,036km) to longer-range services such as: Boston–San Jose (Silicon Valley), a distance of 2,689 miles (4,327km), Boston–Los Angeles, 2,611 miles (4,201km); Los Angeles–Kahului on Maui Island, Hawaii 2,486 miles (4,000km); or Newark, New Jersey–Los Angeles 2,454 miles (3,949km).

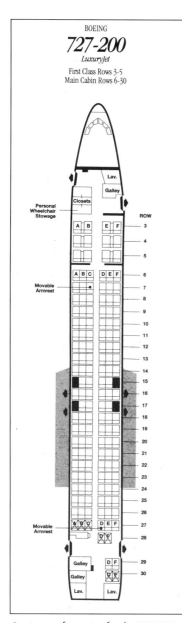

BOEING
727-200
LuxuryJet

First Class Rows 3-5
Main Cabin Rows 6-30

Personal Wheelchair Stowage

Movable Armrest

Movable Armrest

Seating configuration for the 727-200.

Boeing 727

Data:	727-223
First flight:	27 July 1967
Wingspan:	108ft (32.92m)
Wing area:	1,700sq ft (157.9sq m)
Length:	153ft 2in (46.72m)
Height:	34ft (10.37m)
Seating:	3 crew, 150 passengers
Cargo volume:	1,454cu ft (cu m)
Fuel Capacity:	52,700lb (23,926kg)
Empty weight:	101,100lb (45,900kg)
Max take-off weight:	178,000lb (80,812kg)
Range max fuel:	2,400nm (9,450km) (with typical payload)
Range max payload:	2,140nm (2,140km)
Cruising Speed:	515kt (953kph)
Powerplant:	3 x P&W JT8D9A 14,500lb (64.4kN) thrust turbofans
Max ceiling:	42,000ft (12,810m)

First delivery to AA: 25 January 1964
Number 727s bought new by AA: 167 [1]
No in service: 66 (-223)[2], 15 (-227)[3]
[1] 16 in 1964, 13 in 1965, 14 in 1966, 11 in 1967, 27 in 1968, 18 in 1969, 6 in 1975, 10 in 1976, 12 in 1977, 9 in 1978, 9 in 1979, 10 in 1980, 12 in 1981.
[2] 108 -223s bought new 22 in 68, 19 in 1969, 6 in 1975, 10 in 1976, 12 in 1977, 9 in 1978, 8 in 1979, 9 in 1980, 12 in 1981.
[3] Bought from Braniff, 4 in 1980, 11 in 1981.

The Boeing 727 started as a short and medium-range airliner to take up the business that the Boeing 707 could not handle economically. Longlived — it was in production from 1963 to 1984 selling 1,831 units — it was the 'world's favourite airliner' until its short-range stablemate, the Boeing 737, overtook it selling 2,648 aircraft with orders still accruing for the new -700. Boeing's second jet airliner following on from the 707, the 727 started life in the

58

Above: *American still has 81 727s on its inventory, the youngest being at least 16 years old. 727-223 N6821 flew with American from 1968 to 1994.* Peter R. March

mid-1950s. Despite its later success, the early years were difficult with competition from the DC-9, the Caravelle and the Lockheed Electra. Indeed, American, one of the most sought after customers, initially thought that the Electra would solve its requirements, particularly when the cost ($4 million against $2.1 million) was taken into account. However, pragmatically, with a view of the competition interest (both United and Eastern had ordered 727s), American signed a letter of intent for 25 aircraft on 16 May 1961, this becoming a firm order on 10 August 1961. The first 727, N7001U later to go to United, flew on 9 February 1963; the first deliveries — to United and Eastern — took place at the end of 1963 and certification took place in December of the same year. Within two months the first examples were in service. American got its first, N1971, on 25 January 1964; it was the first of more than 200 new and secondhand 727s that would serve with the company, the bulk of which were 727-223s, the designation given to the 727-223s sold to American. The 727-200 is a simple stretched version of the -100 (by 20ft — 10ft before and after the

wing) allowing an extra eight seat rows increasing an all tourist seat arrangement from 120 to 170. But there was no other improvement to engines or tankage — which meant that the -200 had a reduced range because of its increased weight. The -200 was announced in August 1965, rolled-out on 29 June 1967, flew first on 27 July 1967 and was certificated on 30 November 1967. American's initial order was for 22 aircraft, the first of which was N6800. Its first flight was on 20 January 1968 and it was delivered to American a month later. The last, N715AA, was delivered in September 1981. The -227s are ex-Braniff aircraft bought secondhand in the early 1980s. Today the 727s may be showing their age, but they still fulfil a vital role in the American fleet. Their 12 first class and 138 cabin class seating arrangement carries customers over the short ranges — up to around 1,500 miles (2,414km) — on routes such as St Louis–Chicago at the short end (258 miles/415km), to Chicago–Fort Lauderdale (1,182 miles/1,902km) and Newark (New York)–San Juan on Puerto Rico (1,619 miles/1,765km).

Above: *Boeing 727-223 N6811 was delivered to American in May 1968; she was eventually withdrawn in 1994.* Peter R. March

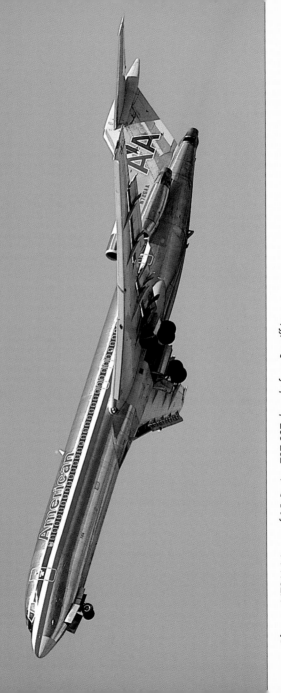

Above: N726AA is one of 15 Boeing 727-227's bought from Braniff in 1980–81. Austin J. Brown

Fokker 100

First flight:	30 November 1986
Wingspan:	92ft 2in (28.08m)
Wing area:	1,006.4sq ft (93.5sq m)
Length:	116ft 7in (35.53m)
Height:	27ft 11in (8.5m)
Seating:	2 crew, 97-122 passengers
Cargo volume:	22,160lb (10,061kg)
Fuel capacity:	23,700lb (10,760kg)
Weight empty:	57,900lb (26,287kg)
Max t/oweight:	98,000lb (44,492kg)
Max Range:	1,710nm (3,167km)
Cruising speed:	430kt (804kph)
Powerplant:	2 x Rolls-Royce Tay Mk 650-15 15,100lb (67.2kN) thrust turbofans
Service ceiling:	35,000ft (10,675m)

First delivery to AA: 11 July 1991
Number bought by AA: 75 (13 in 91, 26 in 92, 23 in 93, 13 in 94)
Number in service end 1996: 75

Designed as an F28 replacement, the Fokker 100 is a stretched, modernised improvement of the original aircraft with a pair of new Rolls-Royce Tay engines. Launched in November 1983, MBB built the midsection and tail and Shorts the wing. The Fokker 100 first flew on 30 November 1986, received certification in November 1987 and the first order — for Swissair — was delivered in February 1988. This excellent short/medium-range airliner was struggling to get orders until American came in for 75 with options on a further 75 with uprated Tay 650s, thus conforming to stage III noise limits. The deliveries started with N1400H and the 75th delivery, N1474D accepted by American on 9 June 1994, was the 250th built — so the Fokker 100 has already outsold its predecessor the F28 family. The Fokker 100s in American service are configured with seating for eight first class and 89 cabin class passengers. They are used mainly on routes up to 1,000 miles.

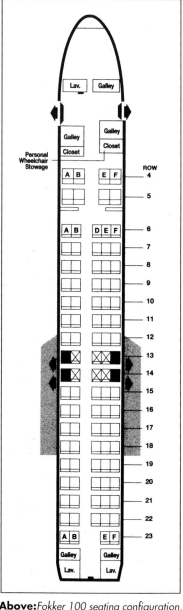

Above: Fokker 100 seating configuration.

62

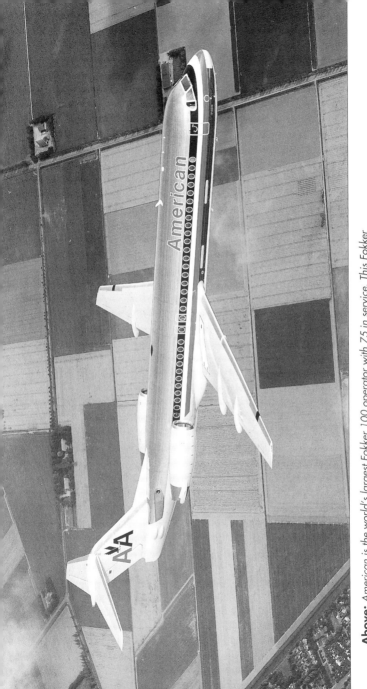

Above: American is the world's largest Fokker 100 operator with 75 in service. This Fokker PR picture shows an American100 over Amsterdam. Aviation Picture Library

Above: MD-11 N1768D was originally destined for Jugoslovenski Aerotransport but the slot wasn't taken up and manufacturer's serial number 48436 became N1768D delivered to American in April 1992. Peter R. March

Below: Superficially a DC-10 derivative, the MD-11 has a new wing (note the winglets), tail and powerplants. Here an MD-11 is loaded at Miami in1994. Peter R. March

Above: *N1757A one of five MD-11s delivered to American in 1991.* Philip J. Birtles

McDonnell Douglas MD-11

First flight:	10 January 1990
Wingspan:	169ft 10in (51.77m)
Wing area:	3,648sq ft (338.9sq m)
Length:	201ft 4in (61.37m)
Height:	57ft 9in (17.6m)
Max seating:	2 crew, 250–405 passengers
Cargo volume:	5,406cu ft (154cu m)
Fuel capacity:	258,100lb (117,177kg)
Empty weight:	304,200lb (138,107kg)
Max take-off weight:	618,000lb (280,572kg)
Range:	6,790nm (12,566km) with 323 passengers
Cruising speed:	456kt (853kph)
Powerplant:	3 x GE CF6-80C2D1F 61,500lb (273.6kN) thrust turbofans
Service ceiling:	42,000ft (12,810m)

First delivery to AA: 1 February 1991
Number bought by AA: 19 (5 in 1991, 6 in 1992, 6 in 1993)
Number in service at end 1996: 16 (of which 2 due for FedEx in 1998)

The McDonnell Douglas MD-11 was launched on 30 December 1986 as a result of a two-year study to find a DC-10 replacement. It first flew on 10 January 1990 and received certification in November 1990. It is very like the DC-10 but with a stretched fuselage (nearly 20ft), winglets, a modified tail, advanced cockpit, restyled cabin and new engines. The MD-11 has not proved to be an outstanding success despite its lead on rival Airbus A330 and Boeing 777 types. As the launch customer for the DC-10, it is not surprising that American would be interested in this improved version and, indeed, American was an early customer for MD-11.

On 7 February 1989 it ordered eight powered by General Electric CF6-80C2D1F engines, with options on another 42. The first three aircraft (N1751A/N1752K/N1750B) were taken over from BA options and therefore allowed American early delivery. There was another order on 12 March 1990 for a further seven (with CF80C2 engines) for delivery in 1991, and

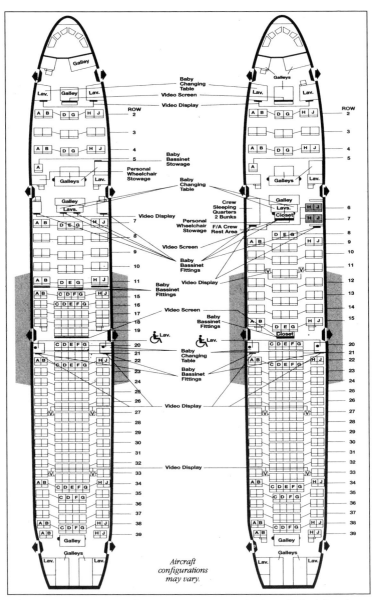

Above: *MD-11 seating configurations — International Atlantic flights left and International Pacific flights right.*

four more were ordered on 11 February 1991. American took delivery of its first, N1751A, on 1 February 1991, with two more in April and May. There were problems with the first aircraft which led to it being withdrawn from service and delivery of subsequent aircraft was delayed pending modifications. Things improved after a few glitches were ironed out (fuel burn, flight-deck computers and air-conditioning) but nevertheless their planned use from 2 March 1991 on a new trans-Pacific service from San Jose to Tokyo, didn't get off the ground — and it was initiated using DC-10-30ERs. MD-11s were also intended for use on Dallas-Tokyo services rather than 747SPs bought in 1986. With 251 seats as against 203 of the 747SP, the MD-11 should have been able to handle these services easily. The beginning of the 1990s saw recession and a reduction in orders which would have given American an overall fleet of 775 aircraft. Particularly hit were the projected 50 MD-11s, and Chairman Robert Crandall announced plans in November 1991 to cut, defer or cancel 93 aircraft including Fokker 100s, 757s and 767s. The MD-11 commitment at the time was 19 firm orders with 31 options. 11 options were cancelled immediately: in the end American went on to cancel more of the MD-11 orders and received only 19 MD-11s. 12 of these are due to be sold to FedEx. Three have already gone (N1751A/N1753/N1754) and three will go in 1997. Today the MD-11s are used on long-haul flights across the Atlantic and the Pacific, such as Seattle–Tokyo (4,769 miles/7,673km), San Jose–Tokyo (5,154 miles/8,293km) and Dallas/Fort Worth–Tokyo (6,427 miles/10,341km). The transatlantic crossings include flights from Chicago to London Heathrow (3,953 miles/6,360km) and Dallas/Fort Worth to London Gatwick (4,771 miles/7,677km). The MD-11 is configured with different seating arrangements for each transoceanic operation — the Atlantic operations split 19 first, 35 business and 203 cabin class; the Pacific split 19–56–163.

Below: *Twelve of American's 19 MD-11s are due to be sold to Federal Express. Here is N1768D in 1996.* Peter R. March

Airbus A300B4-605R

First flight:	28 October 1972 (A300B)
Wingspan:	147ft 1in (44.84m)
Wing area:	2,798.7sq ft (260sq m)
Length:	177ft 5in (54.08m)
Height:	54ft 3in (16.53m)
Seating:	2 crew and 266 passengers
Cargo volume:	22 LD3 containers
Fuel capacity:	120,600lb (54,752kg)
Empty weight:	209,200lb (94, 977kg)
Max take-off weight:	375,890lb (170,654kg)
Max Range:	4,050nm (7,505km) with 266 passengers etc
Cruising speed:	456kt (853kph)
Powerplant:	2 x GE CF6-80C2A5s 61, 500lb/273,6kN thrust
Service ceiling:	42,000ft (12,810m)

First delivery to AA: 20 April 1988
Number bought by AA: 35 (13 in 88, 12 in 89, 5 in 91, 4 in 92, 1 in 93)
Number in service at end 1996: 35

The A300 grew from a European requirement for a wide-bodied jet on medium-range routes. After much discussion between potential partners the Airbus Industrie consortium was created, composed of Aérospatiale 37.9%, Deutsche Aerospace 37.9%, BAe 20% and CASA 4.2%. Fokker and Belairbus were also involved. The prototype A330B1 first flew on 28 October 1972, and this led to the main production version, a slightly stretched version of the prototype, the A300B2. A long-range version — the A300B4 — followed in 1974. In May 1984 the A300B4 ceased production with the A300-600 taking over. It was improved substantially over the earlier models with better aerodynamics, an A310 tail which improved payloads, an EFIS cockpit for two-man operation, winglets, new brakes and a host of other modifications. American was the launch customer for the

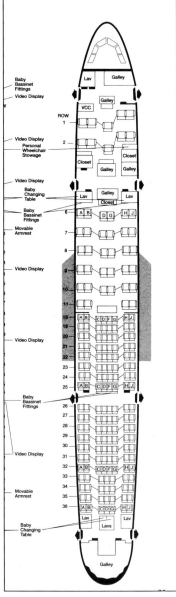

Airbus A300 seating configuration.

68

extended range -600R which has an extra fuel tank in the tail, thus allowing ETOPS transoceanic operations. The American Airbuses were bought for operations to the Caribbean, many of the flights staging through Miami; examples are New York JFK–San Juan, Puerto Rico (3,452 miles/km) and JFK–Montego Bay, Jamaica via Miami (1,090 plus 524 miles/km).

However the Airbuses are also used on flights to Europe, to a variety of destinations, such as Boston–London Heathrow (3,265miles/km) and Boston–Orly (3,448miles/km). The seating arrangements are in two main configurations — 16 first and 251 cabin class totalling 267 seats and 10 first, 34 business and 148 cabin totalling 192.

Above: *Airbus A300B4-605R N33069 seen over Miami in 1992.* Peter R. March

Below: *N70072 seen at London Heathrow 1997.* Philip J. Birtles

AMERICAN EAGLE AIRCRAFT

Above: *The first Simmons ATR-42 was delivered in 1986.* Ian Allan Library

Right: *ATR-42 seating configuration.*

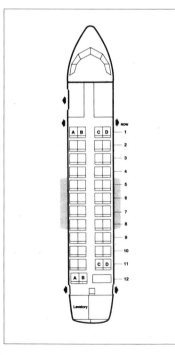

ATR-42-312

First flight:	16 August 1984
Wingspan:	80ft 8in (24.57m)
Length:	74ft 5in (22.67m)
Height:	24ft 11in (7.59m)
Seating:	2 crew, 42-50 passengers
Range:	2,720nm (5,040km) at econ cruise
Cruising speed:	243-265kt (450-490kph)
Powerplant:	2 x P&WCanada 1,800 shp (1,340kW) PW120s driving four-bladed props
Used by:	Executive Airlines, Flagship Airlines
Number in fleet at end 1996:	46, options on 10 more

Formed by Aérospatiale and Aeritalia (now Alenia), Avions de Transport Regional was established to produce regional airliners. The ATR-42 was launched in October 1981, flew first on 16 August 1984, received certification (France and Italy) in September 1985 and entered airline service on 9 December 1985 with Air Littoral. Standard version is the -300; the -320 has PW 21 engines for hot and high conditions.

Above: *ATR72-201 EI-CBC of Executive Airlines.* Austin J. Brown

Below: *ATR-72 seating configuration.*

ATR-72-200

First flight:	27 October 1988
Wingspan:	88ft 9in (27.05m)
Length:	89ft 2in (21.17m)
Height:	25ft 1in (7.65m)
Seating:	2 crew, 62-70 passengers
Range:	1,200nm (2,665km)
Cruising speed:	248-284kt max (460-526kph)
Powerplant:	2 x P&W Canada 2,160shp (1,610kW) PW124B Turboprops driving four bladed props
Used by:	Executive Airlines, Simmons Airlines

Number in fleet at end 1996: 33, with options on 42 more

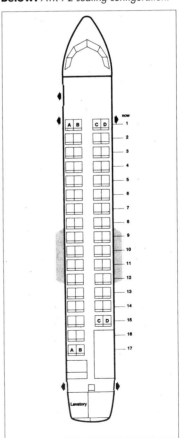

Stretched version of ATR-42 launched January 1986. Certification (France and US) in late 1989. Entered service with Finnair on 27 November 1989. Differences are a 14ft 9in (4.5m) stretch and new wings outboard the engine. Other versions include the 210 optimised for hot and high operations using P&W127 engines for better take-off performance.

Above: *This Shorts 360-200 was leased by Simmons Airlines 1989–93.*
Austin J. Brown

Below: *Shorts 360 seating configuration.*

Shorts 360-200

First flight:	1 June 1981
Wingspan:	74ft 10in (22.8m)
Length:	70ft 10in (21.58m)
Height:	23ft 10in (7.27m)
Seating:	2 crew,
	36–39 passengers
Range:	570nm (1,055km)
Cruising speed:	210kt max (390kph)
Powerplant:	2 x P&WCanada
	1,327shp (990kW)
	PT6A-65R Turboprops
	driving six-bladed props

Used by: Executive Airlines
Number in fleet at end 1996: 16

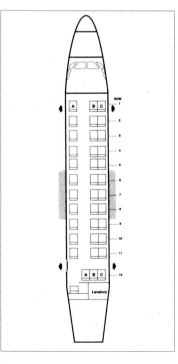

Stretched and improved version of the Shorts 330, the 360 has a longer fuselage allowing 36–39 passengers as against 30, a new tail and rear fuselage, and improved engines. It was certificated on 3 September 1982 and entered service with Suburban Airlines in November of the same year.

Above: *SAAB 340B N227AE of Flagship Airlines.* Austin J. Brown

Below: *SAAB 340B seating configuration.*

SAAB 340B

First flight:	25 January 1983
Wingspan:	70ft 4in (21.44m)
Length:	64ft 9in (19.73m)
Height:	22ft 11in (6.97m)
Seating:	2 crew,
	33–35 passengers
Range:	1,200nm (2,665km)
Cruising speed:	282kt max (526kph)
Powerplant:	2 x GE 1,750shp
	(1,305kW) CT7-9B
	Turboprops driving
	four-bladed props
Used by:	Flagship Airlines,
	Simmons Airlines,
	West Wings Airlines

Number in fleet at end 1996: 117

The SAAB 340B has more powerful engines, a larger tailplane and a higher take-off weight than the earlier 340A. The first 340B was delivered in 1989 and its development — the 340B Plus — has also proved to be a very useful regional airliner.

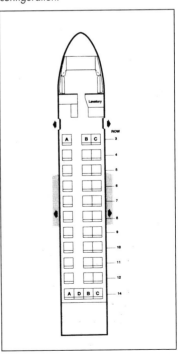

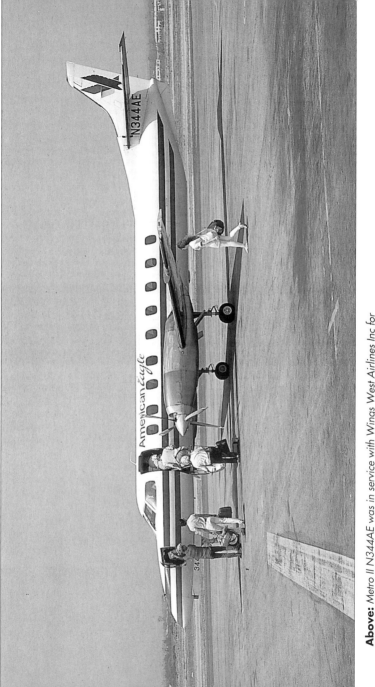

Above: Metro II N344AE was in service with Wings West Airlines Inc for four years from 1989. Austin J. Brown

BAe Jetstream 32

First flight:	17 June 1988
Wingspan:	52ft (15.85m)
Length:	47ft 2in (14.37m)
Height:	17ft 6in (5.37m)
Seating:	2 crew, 19 passengers
Range:	643nm (1,192km)
Cruising speed:	264kt max (490kph)
Powerplant:	2 x Garrett 1,020shp (760kW) TPE331-12UAR Turboprops driving four-bladed props
Used by:	Flagship Airlines, Wings West Airlines

Number in fleet at end 1996: 31

The Jetstream 32, also known as the Super 31, is a significant improvement on its predecessor. Certificated on 7 October 1988, entering service later that month with Big Sky Airlines, the Jetstream 32 is a versatile regional airliner and feeder jet.

Below: *Jetstream Super 31 N951AE has served with Wings West Airlines since 1991. The carrier provides a network of services based on hubs at Los Angeles and Dallas/Fort Worth. Wings West Airlines operates three Super 31s.*
Austin J. Brown

Above and Below: *DC-10s seen at Los Angeles International Airport in May 1993. LAX plays an important part of American's operations: scheduled flights leave for a variety of domestic and international destinations, the latter including Amsterdam, Auckland, Buenos Aires and other Central and South American cities, the Caribbean, London (Gatwick and Heathrow), Johannesburg and other South African cities, Milan, Naples, Paris, Quebec and Zurich.* Leo Marriott

American Airlines Aircraft Fleet List

Reg.	Aircraft Type	Notes/Names	Reg.	Aircraft Type	Notes/Names
			N152AA	Douglas DC-10-10	leased to Hawaiian AL
			N153AA	Douglas DC-10-10	leased to Hawaiian AL

Douglas DC-10

Reg.	Aircraft Type	Notes/Names	Reg.	Aircraft Type	Notes/Names
N102AA	Douglas DC-10-10	stored Amarillo	N161AA	Douglas DC-10-10	leased from Polaris to Hawaiian AL
N105AA	Douglas DC-10-10	stored Amarillo			
N106AA	Douglas DC-10-10	stored Amarillo			
N107AA	Douglas DC-10-10	stored Amarillo	N162AA	Douglas DC-10-10	leased to Hawaiian AL
N108AA	Douglas DC-10-10	stored Amarillo			
N112AA	Douglas DC-10-10	stored Amarillo	N163AA	Douglas DC-10 30	leased from Polaris
N115AA	Douglas DC-10-10	stored Amarillo			
N116AA	Douglas DC-10-10	leased to Hawaiian AL	N164AA	Douglas DC-10 30	
			N166AA	Douglas DC-10-10	stored Amarillo
N118AA	Douglas DC-10-10	stored Amarillo	N167AA	Douglas DC-10-10	
N119AA	Douglas DC-10-10	leased to Hawaiian AL	N168AA	Douglas DC-10-10	
			N171AA	Douglas DC-10-10	leased to Hawaiian AL
N120AA	Douglas DC-10-10	stored Amarillo			
N121AA	Douglas DC-10-10	stored Amarillo			
N122AA	Douglas DC-10-10	leased to Hawaiian AL			

McDonnell Douglas MD-80

Reg.	Aircraft Type	Notes/Names	Reg.	Aircraft Type	Notes/Names
N126AA	Douglas DC-10-10				
N127AA	Douglas DC-10-10	stored Amarillo	N203AA	McDonnell Douglas MD-82	
N128AA	Douglas DC-10-10		N205AA	McDonnell Douglas MD-82	
N129AA	Douglas DC-10-10		N207AA	McDonnell Douglas MD-82	leased from Orix
N130AA	Douglas DC-10-10				
N131AA	Douglas DC-10-10		N208AA	McDonnell Douglas MD-82	
N132AA	Douglas DC-10-10		N210AA	McDonnell Douglas MD-82	
N133AA	Doulas DC-10-10		N214AA	McDonnell Douglas MD-82	
N134AA	Douglas DC-10-10		N215AA	McDonnell Douglas MD-82	
N135AA	Douglas DC-10-10		N216AA	McDonnell Douglas MD-82	leased from Orix
N137AA	Dougas DC-10 30				
N140AA	Douglas DC-10 30	leased to Transaero	N218AA	McDonnell Douglas MD-82	
			N219AA	McDonnell Douglas MD-82	
N141AA	Douglas DC-10 30	leased to Transaero	N221AA	McDonnell Douglas MD-82	
			N223AA	McDonnell Douglas MD-82	
N142AA	Douglas DC-10 30	leased to Transaero	N224AA	McDonnell Douglas MD-82	
			N225AA	McDonnell Douglas MD-82	
N143AA	Douglas DC-10 30		N226AA	McDonnell Douglas MD-82	
N144AA	Douglas DC-10 30		N227AA	McDonnell Douglas MD-82	
N146AA	Douglas DC-10-10	stored Amarillo	N228AA	McDonnell Douglas MD-82	
N147AA	Dougas DC-10-10		N232AA	McDonnell Douglas MD-82	
N148AA	Douglas DC-10-10	leased to Hawaiian AL	N233AA	McDonnell Douglas MD-82	
			N234AA	McDonnell Douglas MD-82	
N151AA	Douglas DC-10-10	leased to Hawaiian AL	N236AA	McDonnell Douglas MD-82	
			N237AA	McDonnell Douglas MD-82	

Reg.	Aircraft Type	Reg.	Aircraft Type
N241AA	McDonnell Douglas MD-82	N287AA	McDonnell Douglas MD-82
N242AA	McDonnell Douglas MD-82	N288AA	McDonnell Douglas MD-82
N244AA	McDonnell Douglas MD-82	N289AA	McDonnell Douglas MD-82
N245AA	McDonnell Douglas MD-82	N290AA	McDonnell Douglas MD-82
N246AA	McDonnell Douglas MD-82	N291A	McDonnell Douglas MD-82
N248AA	McDonnell Douglas MD-82	N292AA	McDonnell Douglas MD-82
N249AA	McDonnell Douglas MD-82	N293AA	McDonnell Douglas MD-82
N251AA	McDonnell Douglas MD-82	N294AA	McDonnell Douglas MD-82
N253AA	McDonnell Douglas MD-82	N295AA	McDonnell Douglas MD-82
N255AA	McDonnell Douglas MD-82	N296AA	McDonnell Douglas MD-82
N258AA	McDonnell Douglas MD-82	N297AA	McDonnell Douglas MD-82
N259AA	McDonnell Douglas MD-82	N298AA	McDonnell Douglas MD-82
N262AA	McDonnell Douglas MD-82	N400AA	McDonnell Douglas MD-82
N266AA	McDonnell Douglas MD-82	N402A	McDonnell Douglas MD-82
N269AA	McDonnell Douglas MD-82	N403A	McDonnell Douglas MD-82
N271A	McDonnell Douglas MD-82	N405A	McDonnell Douglas MD-82
N274AA	McDonnell Douglas MD-82	N406A	McDonnell Douglas MD-82
N275AA	McDonnell Douglas MD-82	N407AA	McDonnell Douglas MD-82
N276AA	McDonnell Douglas MD-82	N408AA	McDonnell Douglas MD-82
N278AA	McDonnell Douglas MD-82	N409AA	McDonnell Douglas MD-82
N279AA	McDonnell Douglas MD-82	N410AA	McDonnell Douglas MD-82
N283AA	McDonnell Douglas MD-82	N411AA	McDonnell Douglas MD-82
N285AA	McDonnell Douglas MD-82	N412AA	McDonnell Douglas MD-82
N286AA	McDonnell Douglas MD-82		leased from GECC

Below: *MD-82 seen taking-off from LAX in 1993.* Leo Marriott

Reg.	Aircraft Type	Reg.	Aircraft Type
N413AA	McDonnell Douglas MD-82	N467AA	McDonnell Douglas MD-82
N414AA	McDonnell Douglas MD-82	N468AA	McDonnell Douglas MD-82
N415AA	McDonnell Douglas MD-82	N469AA	McDonnell Douglas MD-82
N416AA	McDonnell Douglas MD-82	N470AA	McDonnell Douglas MD-82
N417AA	McDonnell Douglas MD-82	N471AA	McDonnell Douglas MD-82
N418AA	McDonnell Douglas MD-82	N472AA	McDonnell Douglas MD-82
N419AA	McDonnell Douglas MD-82	N473AA	McDonnell Douglas MD-82
N420AA	McDonnell Douglas MD-82	N474	McDonnell Douglas MD-82
	leased from GECC	N475AA	McDonnell Douglas MD-82
N422AA	McDonnell Douglas MD-82	N476AA	McDonnell Douglas MD-82
	leased from GECC	N477AA	McDonnell Douglas MD-82
N423AA	McDonnell Douglas MD-82	N478AA	McDonnell Douglas MD-82
N424AA	McDonnell Douglas MD-82	N479AA	McDonnell Douglas MD-82
N426AA	McDonnell Douglas MD-82	N480AA	McDonnell Douglas MD-82
N427AA	McDonnell Douglas MD-82	N481AA	McDonnell Douglas MD-82
N428AA	McDonnell Douglas MD-82	N482AA	McDonnell Douglas MD-82
N429AA	McDonnell Douglas MD-82	N483A	McDonnell Douglas MD-82
N430AA	McDonnell Douglas MD-82	N484AA	McDonnell Douglas MD-82
N431AA	McDonnell Douglas MD-82	N485AA	McDonnell Douglas MD-82
N432A	McDonnell Douglas MD-82	N486AA	McDonnell Douglas MD-82
N440AA	McDonnell Douglas MD-82	N487AA	McDonnell Douglas MD-82
N441AA	McDonnell Douglas MD-82	N488AA	McDonnell Douglas MD-82
N442AA	McDonnell Douglas MD-82	N489AA	McDonnell Douglas MD-82
N443AA	McDonnell Douglas MD-82	N490AA	McDonnell Douglas MD-82
	leased from GECC	N491AA	McDonnell Douglas MD-82
N445AA	McDonnell Douglas MD-82	N492AA	McDonnell Douglas MD-82
N446AA	McDonnell Douglas MD-82	N493AA	McDonnell Douglas MD-82
N447A	McDonnell Douglas MD-82	N494AA	McDonnell Douglas MD-82
N448AA	McDonnell Douglas MD-82	N495AA	McDonnell Douglas MD-82
N449AA	McDonnell Douglas MD-82	N496AA	McDonnell Douglas MD-82
N450AA	McDonnell Douglas MD-82	N497AA	McDonnell Douglas MD-82
N451AA	McDonnell Douglas MD-82	N498A	McDonnell Douglas MD-82
N452AA	McDonnell Douglas MD-82	N499AA	McDonnell Douglas MD-82
N453AA	McDonnell Douglas MD-82	N501AM	McDonnell Douglas MD-82
N454AA	McDonnell Douglas MD-82	N513A	McDonnell Douglas MD-82
N455AA	McDonnell Douglas MD-82	N516AM	McDonnell Douglas MD-82
N456AA	McDonnell Douglas MD-82	N552AA	McDonnell Douglas MD-82
N457AA	McDonnell Douglas MD-82	N553A	McDonnell Douglas MD-82
N458AA	McDonnell Douglas MD-82	N554AA	McDonnell Douglas MD-82
N459AA	McDonnell Douglas MD-82	N555AN	McDonnell Douglas MD-82
N460AA	McDonnell Douglas MD-82	N556AA	McDonnell Douglas MD-82
N461AA	McDonnell Douglas MD-82	N557AN	McDonnell Douglas MD-82
N462AA	McDonnell Douglas MD-82	N558AA	McDonnell Douglas MD-82
N463AA	McDonnell Douglas MD-82	N559AA	McDonnell Douglas MD-82
N464AA	McDonnell Douglas MD-82	N560AA	McDonnell Douglas MD-82
N465A	McDonnell Douglas MD-82	N561AA	McDonnell Douglas MD-82
N466AA	McDonnell Douglas MD-82	N573AA	McDonnell Douglas MD-82

Reg.	Aircraft Type	Reg.	Aircraft Type
N574AA	McDonnell Douglas MD-82	N7546A	McDonnell Douglas MD-82
N575AM	McDonnell Douglas MD-82	N7547A	McDonnell Douglas MD-82
N576AA	McDonnell Douglas MD-82	N7548A	McDonnell Douglas MD-82
N577AA	McDonnell Douglas MD-82	N7549A	McDonnell Douglas MD-82
N578AA	McDonnell Douglas MD-82	N7550	McDonnell Douglas MD-82
N579AA	McDonnell Douglas MD-82	N14551	McDonnell Douglas MD-82
N580AA	McDonnell Douglas MD-82	N14545	McDonnell Douglas MD-82
N581AA	McDonnell Douglas MD-82	N33414	McDonnell Douglas MD-82
N582AA	McDonnell Douglas MD-82	N33502	McDonnell Douglas MD-82
N583AA	McDonnell Douglas MD-82	N44503	McDonnell Douglas MD-82
N584AA	McDonnell Douglas MD-82	N59523	McDonnell Douglas MD-82
N585AA	McDonnell Douglas MD-82	N70401	McDonnell Douglas MD-82
N586AA	McDonnell Douglas MD-82	N70404	McDonnell Douglas MD-82
N587AA	McDonnell Douglas MD-82	N70425	McDonnell Douglas MD-82
N3507A	McDonnell Douglas MD-82	N70504	McDonnell Douglas MD-82
N3515	McDonnell Douglas MD-82	N70424	McDonnell Douglas MD-82
N7506	McDonnell Douglas MD-82	N70429	McDonnell Douglas MD-82
N7508	McDonnell Douglas MD-82	N70444	McDonnell Douglas MD-82
N7509	McDonnell Douglas MD-82	N76200	McDonnell Douglas MD-82
N7512A	McDonnell Douglas MD-82	N76201	McDonnell Douglas MD-82
N7514A	McDonnell Douglas MD-82	N76202	McDonnell Douglas MD-82
N7517A	McDonnell Douglas MD-82	N77421	McDonnell Douglas MD-82
N7518A	McDonnell Douglas MD-82		leased from GECC
N7519A	McDonnell Douglas MD-82	N90511	McDonnell Douglas MD-82
N7520A	McDonnell Douglas MD-82		
N7521A	McDonnell Douglas MD-82	N433AA	McDonnell Douglas MD-83
N7522A	McDonnell Douglas MD-82	N434AA	McDonnell Douglas MD-83
N7525A	McDonnell Douglas MD-82	N435AA	McDonnell Douglas MD-83
N7526A	McDonnell Douglas MD-82	N436AA	McDonnell Douglas MD-83
N7527A	McDonnell Douglas MD-82	N437AA	McDonnell Douglas MD-83
N7528A	McDonnell Douglas MD-82	N438AA	McDonnell Douglas MD-83
N7530	McDonnell Douglas MD-82	N439AA	McDonnell Douglas MD-83
N7531A	McDonnell Douglas MD-82	N562AA	McDonnell Douglas MD-83
N7532A	McDonnell Douglas MD-82	N563AA	McDonnell Douglas MD-83
N7533A	McDonnell Douglas MD-82	N564AA	McDonnell Douglas MD-83
N7534A	McDonnell Douglas MD-82	N565AA	McDonnell Douglas MD-83
N7535A	McDonnell Douglas MD-82	N566AA	McDonnell Douglas MD-83
N7536A	McDonnell Douglas MD-82	N567AM	McDonnell Douglas MD-83
N7537A	McDonnell Douglas MD-82	N568AA	McDonnell Douglas MD-83
N7538A	McDonnell Douglas MD-82	N569AA	McDonnell Douglas MD-83
N7539A	McDonnell Douglas MD-82	N570AA	McDonnell Douglas MD-83
N7540A	McDonnell Douglas MD-82	N571AA	McDonnell Douglas MD-83
N7541A	McDonnell Douglas MD-82	N572AA	McDonnell Douglas MD-83
N7542A	McDonnell Douglas MD-82	N588AA	McDonnell Douglas MD-83
N7543A	McDonnell Douglas MD-82	N589AA	McDonnell Douglas MD-83
N7544A	McDonnell Douglas MD-82	N590AA	McDonnell Douglas MD-83
N7545A	McDonnell Douglas MD-82	N591AA	McDonnell Douglas MD-83

Reg.	Aircraft Type	Reg.	Aircraft Type
N592AA	McDonnell Douglas MD-83	N596AA	McDonnell Douglas MD-83
N593AA	McDonnell Douglas MD-83	N597AA	McDonnell Douglas MD-83
N594AA	McDonnell Douglas MD-83	N598AA	McDonnell Douglas MD-83
N595AA	McDonnell Douglas MD-83	N599AA	McDonnell Douglas MD-83

Below: *Another MD-82 departure from LAX in 1993.* Leo Marriott

Boeing 767

Reg.	Aircraft Type	Reg.	Aircraft Type	Reg.	Aircraft Type
		N3018AA	Boeing 767-223	N324AA	Boeing 767-223ER
		N312AA	Boeing 767-223	N325AA	Boeing 767-223ER
		N313AA	Boeing 767-223	N326AA	Boeing 767-223ER
		N315AA	Boeing 767-223ER	N327AA	Boeing 767-223ER
N301AA	Boeing 767-223	N316AA	Boeing 767-223ER	N328AA	Boeing 767-223ER
N302AA	Boeing 767-223	N317AA	Boeing 767-223ER	N329AA	Boeing 767-223ER
N303AA	Boeing 767-223	N319AA	Boeing 767-223ER	N330AA	Boeing 767-223ER
N304AA	Boeing 767-223	N320AA	Boeing 767-223ER	N332AA	Boeing 767-223ER
N305AA	Boeing 767-223	N321AA	Boeing 767-223ER	N334AA	Boeing 767-223ER
N306AA	Boeing 767-223	N322AA	Boeing 767-223ER		leased from GECC
N307AA	Boeing 767-223	N323AA	Boeing 767-223ER	N335AA	Boeing 767-223ER

This page and Right: *American has over 60 ETOPS-rated 767-223ERs and -323ERs. American Airlines was one of the leading pioneers in the development of ETOPS services starting with 767 flights between Switzerland and Chicago on 1 April 1986. This service was soon followed by Dallas–Frankfurt and Dallas-London services using -200ERs.* Leo Marriott, Austin J. Brown (below right)

Reg.	Aircraft Type	Reg.	Aircraft Type	Reg.	Aircraft Type
N336AA	Boeing 767-223ER			N645AA	Boeing 757-223
N338AA	Boeing 767-223ER			N646AA	Boeing 757-223
N339AA	Boeing 767-223ER			N647AA	Boeing 757-223
N351AA	Boeing 767-323ER			N648AA	Boeing 757-223
N352AA	Boeing 767-323ER	N601AN	Boeing 757-223	N649AA	Boeing 757-223
N353AA	Boeing 767-323ER	N602AN	Boeing 757-223	N650AA	Boeing 757-223
N354AA	Boeing 767-323ER	N603AA	Boeing 757-223	N652AA	Boeing 757-223
N355AA	Boeing 767-323ER	N604AA	Boeing 757-223	N653A	Boeing 757-223
N357AA	Boeing 767-323ER	N605AA	Boeing 757-223	N654A	Boeing 757-223
N358AA	Boeing 767-323ER	N606AM	Boeing 757-223	N655AA	Boeing 757-223
	leased from GECC	N607AM	Boeing 757-223	N656AA	Boeing 757-223
N359AA	Boeing 767-323ER	N608AA	Boeing 757-223	N657AM	Boeing 757-223
N360AA	Boeing 767-323ER	N609AA	Boeing 757-223	N658AA	Boeing 757-223
N361AA	Boeing 767-323ER	N610AA	Boeing 757-223	N659AA	Boeing 757-223
N362AA	Boeing 767-323ER	N611AM	Boeing 757-223		Pride of American
N363AA	Boeing 767-323ER	N612AA	Boeing 757-223	N660AM	Boeing 757-223
	leased from GECC	N613AA	Boeing 757-223	N661AA	Boeing 757-223
N366AA	Boeing 767-323ER	N614AA	Boeing 757-223	N662AA	Boeing 757-223
N368AA	Boeing 767-323ER	N615AM	Boeing 757-223	N663AM	Boeing 757-223
N369AA	Boeing 767-323ER	N616AA	Boeing 757-223	N664AA	Boeing 757-223
N370AA	Boeing 767-323ER	N618AA	Boeing 757-223	N665AA	Boeing 757-223
N371AA	Boeing 767-323ER	N619AA	Boeing 757-223	N666A	Boeing 757-223
N372AA	Boeing 767-323ER	N620AA	Boeing 757-223	N668AA	Boeing 757-223
N373AA	Boeing 767-323ER	N621AM	Boeing 757-223	N669AA	Boeing 757-223
N374AA	Boeing 767-323ER	N622AA	Boeing 757-223	N670AA	Boeing 757-223
N376AN	Boeing 767-323ER	N623AA	Boeing 757-223	N671AA	Boeing 757-223
N377AN	Boeing 767-323ER	N624AA	Boeing 757-223	N672AA	Boeing 757-223
N378AN	Boeing 767-323ER	N625AA	Boeing 757-223	N681AA	Boeing 757-223
N379AA	Boeing 767-323ER	N626AA	Boeing 757-223	N682AA	Boeing 757-223
N380AN	Boeing 767-323ER	N627AA	Boeing 757-223	N683A	Boeing 757-223
N381AN	Boeing 767-323ER	N628AA	Boeing 757-223	N684AA	Boeing 757-223
N382AN	Boeing 767-323ER	N629AA	Boeing 757-223	N685AA	Boeing 757-223
N383AN	Boeing 767-323ER	N630AA	Boeing 757-223	N686AA	Boeing 757-223
N384AA	Boeing 767-323ER	N631AA	Boeing 757-223	N687AA	Boeing 757-223
N385AM	Boeing 767-323ER	N632AA	Boeing 757-223	N688AA	Boeing 757-223
N386AA	Boeing 767-323ER	N633AA	Boeing 757-223	N689AA	Boeing 757-223
N387AM	Boeing 767-323ER	N634AA	Boeing 757-223	N690AA	Boeing 757-223
N388AA	Boeing 767-323ER	N635AA	Boeing 757-223	N691AA	Boeing 757-223
N389AA	Boeing 767-323ER	N636AM	Boeing 757-223	N692AA	Boeing 757-223
N390AA	Boeing 767-323ER	N637AM	Boeing 757-223	N693AA	Boeing 757-223
N391AA	Boeing 767-323ER	N638AA	Boeing 757-223	N694AN	Boeing 757-223
N7375A	Boeing 767-323ER	N639AA	Boeing 757-223	N695AN	Boeing 757-223
N39356	Boeing 767-323ER	N640A	Boeing 757-223	N696AN	Boeing 757-223
N39364	Boeing 767-323ER	N641AA	Boeing 757-223		
N39365	Boeing 767-323ER	N642AA	Boeing 757-223		
N39367	Boeing 767-323ER	N643AA	Boeing 757-223		
		N644AA	Boeing 757-223		

Boeing 757

Reg.	Aircraft Type	Reg.	Aircraft Type	Reg.	Aircraft Type
N697AN	Boeing 757-223	N705AA	Boeing 727-223	N843AA	Boeing 727-223
N698AN	Boeing 757-223	N706AA	Boeing 727-223		stored Amarillo
N699AN	Boeing 757-223		Leased from GECC	N844AA	Boeing 727-223
N7667A	Boeing 757-223	N707AA	Boeing 727-223	N845AA	Boeing 727-223
			Leased from GECC		stored Amarillo
N677AA	Boeing 757-3A4	N708AA	Boeing 727-223	N846AA	Boeing 727-223
N678AA	Boeing 757-3A4		Leased from GECC	N847AA	Boeing 727-223
N679AA	Boeing 757-3A4	N709AA	Boeing 727-223		Leased from GECC
N680AA	Boeing 757-3A4		Leased from GECC	N848AA	Boeing 727-223
		N710AA	Boeing 727-223		Leased from GECC
			Leased from GECC	N849AA	Boeing 727-223
		N712AA	Boeing 727-223		Leased from GECC
			Leased from GECC	N850AA	Boeing 727-223
		N713AA	Boeing 727-223		Leased from GECC
N701AA	Boeing 727-223		Leased from GECC	N858AA	Boeing 727-223
N702AA	Boeing 727-223	N715AA	Boeing 727-223	N859AA	Boeing 727-223
N703AA	Boeing 727-223		Leased from GECC	N860AA	Boeing 727-223

Boeing 727

Below: *American Airlines took delivery of its first 727-223 on 20 January 1968 for use as a short and medium range airliner. The aircraft continued in production until 1984 and was widely considered the 'world's favourite airliner' until overtaken by its more modern sister, the Boeing 737.* Austin J. Brown

Reg.	Aircraft Type	Reg.	Aircraft Type	Reg.	Aircraft Type
N861AA	Boeing 727-223	N882AA	Boeing 727-223	N716AA	Boeing 727-227
N862AA	Boeing 727-223	N883AA	Boeing 727-223	N717AA	Boeing 727-227
N863AA	Boeing 727-223	N884AA	Boeing 727-223	N718AA	Boeing 727-227
N864AA	Boeing 727-223	N885AA	Boeing 727-223	N719AA	Boeing 727-227
N865AA	Boeing 727-223	N886A	Boeing 727-223	N720AA	Boeing 727-227
N866AA	Boeing 727-223	N887AA	Boeing 727-223	N721AA	Boeing 727-227
N867AA	Boeing 727-223	N889AA	Boeing 727-223	N722AA	Boeing 727-227
N868AA	Boeing 727-223	N890AA	Boeing 727-223	N723AA	Boeing 727-227
N870AA	Boeing 727-223	N891A	Boeing 727-223	N725AA	Boeing 727-227
N871AA	Boeing 727-223	N892AA	Boeing 727-223	N726AA	Boeing 727-227
N872AA	Boeing 727-223	N893AA	Boeing 727-223	N727AA	Boeing 727-227
N873AA	Boeing 727-223	N894AA	Boeing 727-223	N728AA	Boeing 727-227
N874AA	Boeing 727-223	N895AA	Boeing 727-223	N729AA	Boeing 727-227
N875AA	Boeing 727-223	N896AA	Boeing 727-223	N730AA	Boeing 727-227
N876AA	Boeing 727-223	N897AA	Boeing 727-223	N731AA	Boeing 727-227
N877AA	Boeing 727-223	N898AA	Boeing 727-223		
N878AA	Boeing 727-223	N899AA	Boeing 727-223		
N879AA	Boeing 727-223	N6813	Boeing 727-223	**Fokker 100**	
N880AA	Boeing 727-223	N6818	Boeing 727-223		
N881AA	Boeing 727-223	N681	Boeing 727-223	N1400H	Fokker 100
		N6822	Boeing 727-223	N1401G	Fokker 100
		N6823	Boeing 727-223	N1402K	Fokker 100
		N6835	Boeing 727-223	N1403M	Fokker 100

Below: *N727AA was one of the 727-227s bought by American from Braniff in the early 1980s.* Leo Marriott

Reg.	Aircraft Type	Reg.	Aircraft Type	Reg.	Aircraft Type
N1404D	Fokker 100	N1428D	Fokker 100	N1452B	Fokker 100
N1405J	Fokker 100	N1429G	Fokker 100	N1453D	Fokker 100
N1406A	Fokker 100	N1430D	Fokker 100	N1454D	Fokker 100
N1407D	Fokker 100	N1431B	Fokker 100	N1455K	Fokker 100
N1408B	Fokker 100	N1432A	Fokker 100	N1456D	Fokker 100
N1409B	Fokker 100	N1433B	Fokker 100	N1457B	Fokker 100
N1410E	Fokker 100	N1434A	Fokker 100	N1458H	Fokker 100
N1411G	Fokker 100	N1435D	Fokker 100	N1459A	Fokker 100
N1412A	Fokker 100	N1436A	Fokker 100	N1460A	Fokker 100
N1413A	Fokker 100	N1437A	Fokker 100	N1461C	Fokker 100
N1414D	Fokker 100	N1438B	Fokker 100	N1462C	Fokker 100
N1415K	Fokker 100	N1439A	Fokker 100	N1463A	Fokker 100
N1416A	Fokker 100	N1440A	Fokker 100	N1464A	Fokker 100
N1417D	Fokker 100	N1441A	Fokker 100	N1465K	Fokker 100
N1418A	Fokker 100	N1442E	Fokker 100	N1466A	Fokker 100
N1419D	Fokker 100	N1443A	Fokker 100	N1467A	Fokker 100
N1420D	Fokker 100	N1444N	Fokker 100	N1468A	Fokker 100
N1421K	Fokker 100	N1445B	Fokker 100	N1469D	Fokker 100
N1422J	Fokker 100	N1446A	Fokker 100	N1470K	Fokker 100
N1423A	Fokker 100	N1447L	Fokker 100	N1471G	Fokker 100
N1424M	Fokker 100	N1448A	Fokker 100	N1472B	Fokker 100
N1425A	Fokker 100	N1449D	Fokker 100	N1473K	Fokker 100
N1426A	Fokker 100	N1450A	Fokker 100	N1474D	Fokker 100
N1427A	Fokker 100	N1451N	Fokker 100		

Below: *The 767 was introduced in 1982, some 11 years after the inaugural DC-10 service. Both types are pictured here, the 767-223 leading.* Philip J. Birtles

Above: *MD-83 N596AA over Washington National, May 1996.* Philip Birtles

Reg.	Aircraft Type	Reg.	Aircraft Type
McDonnell Douglas MD-11		N11060	Airbus A300B4-605R
		N14053	Airbus A300B4- 605R
		N14056	Airbus A300B4-605R
N1750B	McDonnell Douglas MD-11	N14061	Airbus A300B4-605R
	for Federal Express	N14065	Airbus A300B4-605R
N1752K	McDonnell Douglas MD-11	N14068	Airbus A300B4-605R
	for Federal Express	N14077	Airbus A300B4-605R
N1755	McDonnell Douglas MD-11	N18066	Airbus A300B4-605R
N1756	McDonnell Douglas MD-11		leased from GECC
N1757A	McDonnell Douglas MD-11	N19059	Airbus A300B4-605R
N1758B	McDonnell Douglas MD-11		leased from GECC
N1759	McDonnell Douglas MD-11	N25071	Airbus A300B4-605R
N1760A	McDonnell Douglas MD-11		leased from GECC
N1761R	McDonnell Douglas MD-11	N33069	Airbus A300B4-605R
N1762B	McDonnell Douglas MD-11	N34078	Airbus A300B4-605R
N1763	McDonnell Douglas MD-11	N40064	Airbus A300B4-605R
N1764B	McDonnell Douglas MD-11	N41063	Airbus A300B4-605R
N1765B	McDonnell Douglas MD-11	N50051	Airbus A300B4-605R
N1766A	McDonnell Douglas MD-11	N59081	Airbus A300B4-605R
N1767A	McDonnell Douglas MD-11	N70054	Airbus A300B4-605R
N1768D	McDonnell Douglas MD-11	N70072	Airbus A300B4-605R
			leased from Orix
		N70073	Airbus A300B4-605R
Airbus A300B4-605R			leased from GECC
		N70074	Airbus A300B4-605R
		N70079	Airbus A300B4-605R
		N7080	Airbus A300B4-605R
N3075A	Airbus A300B4-605R	N80052	Airbus A300B4-605R
N7055A	Airbus A300B4-605R	N80057	Airbus A300B4-605R
	leased from GECC		leased from GECC
N7062A	Airbus A300B4-605R	N80058	Airbus A300B4-605R
N7076A	Airbus A300B4-605R	N80084	Airbus A300B4-605R
N7082A	Airbus A300B4-605R	N90070	Airbus A300B4-605R
N7083A	Airbus A300B4-605R		leased from Orix
N8067A	Airbus A300B4-605R	N91050	Airbus A300B4-605R

Above: *American bought Airbus A300s in 1987 for use on its Caribbean services.* Leo Marriott

Below: *MD-82 N464AA — one of the massive 1984 order.* Peter R. March

Above: *DC-10s taxiing at Dallas/Fort Worth.* Peter R. March

Below: *American's largest hub is at Dallas/Fort Worth and will only get bigger. Here an 727-223 (foreground) and 767s at gates 26–28.* Peter R. March

Engineering

Engineering

Every aircraft is checked regularly in order to maintain strict safety in the air. As with all airline companies American is very aware of its responsibilities and checks its aircraft in a logical and thorough manner learning from its maintenance mistakes. These are the main checks that take place.

'PS' Check

Every aircraft is checked regularly every day in its PS (Periodic Service) Check. This begins with a visual inspection. The log book is then checked for entries and maintenance needs. The PS check can be performed overnight or during downtime during the flight day. It averages approximately two man-hours.

'A' Checks

The 'A' Check is more detailed than the daily PS check. It is performed roughly once a week, which averages every 60 flight hours. The 'A' check is carried out at one of 39 stations around the American system. It averages 10-20 man-hours.

'B' Checks

The 'B' check is a more thorough maintenance check, carried out approximately once a month, roughly every 300-500 flight hours. Besides a specific service performed on the aircraft, a detailed series of systems and operational checks are run through. The company carries out 'B' checks inside one of its hangars at six different cities around the system. A 'B' check requires approximately 100 man-hours.

Above: *A complicated set of manoeuvres! Two DC-10s, an MD-83 and a Boeing 767 at Dallas/Fort Worth.* Peter R. March

'C' Checks

The 'C' check is the most intensive type of maintenance work. The airframe (virtually the entire aircraft), is put through an exhaustive series of checks, inspections and overhaul work, carried out at one of American's heavy maintenance and engineering centres in Tulsa, Oklahoma, or Fort Worth. The 'C' check varies with the type of aircraft — narrow-bodied or wide-bodied. Narrow-bodied aircraft have two types of check — a 'Light C' check once a year, taking approximately 2,100 man-hours, and every fourth 'C' check a 'Heavy C' check of 20,000-30,000 man hours. Because of the complexity of the aircraft, all wide-bodied inspections are 'Heavy C' checks. This is performed every 15-18 months, and takes approximately 10,000 man-hours and two weeks to complete.

'C' Check Locations by Aircraft Type.

Tulsa — McDonnell Douglas aircraft: MD-11, DC-10, MD-80s.
Fokker Aircraft: F100.
Boeing Aircraft: 727.
Fort Worth — Boeing: 767, 757.

Jet Engine Overhaul

Jet engines are not overhauled after a specific number of hours, but are monitored continually inside and out and serviced when necessary. This is carried out at Tulsa and Fort Worth, Tulsa handling all General Electric and Pratt-Whitney jet engine work, and Fort Worth the Rolls-Royce jet engines. Engine replacement is carried out at one of the six 'B' check hangar locations around the country.

Below: *MD-80s — like this MD-82, N497AA at Washington — are given their intensive 'C' checks at Tulsa, Oklahoma.* Peter R. March

Interesting Facts and Figures

Top Ten Record Passenger Days (as of 1/9/96)

No.	Passenger Miles	Load Factor	Date
1.	377,260,000	83.6%	30/6/95
2.	372,000,000	83.2%	1/8/92
3.	368,900,000	83.5%	16/8/92
4.	367,514,000	84.1%	7/7/96
5.	367,000,000	83.0%	2/8/92
6.	364,952,000	81.5%	22/12/95
7.	364,900,000	79,7%	31/7/93
8.	364,800,000	82.2%	21/12/95
9.	364,200,000	82,6%	15/8/92
10.	363,900,000	82.2%	31/7/92

Below: *N848AE Jetstream Super 31 was delivered to American Eagle in September 1989 and ran with Flagship Airlines.* BAe

Top Five System Record Load Factor Days (as of 1/9/96)

No.	Load Factor	Date
1.	87.8%	28/11/82
2.	87.2%	25/11/79
3.	86.9%	22/4/79
4.	86.6%	25/3/83
5.	86.4%	23/5/85

Top Five Mainland US Record Load Factor Days (as of 1/9/96)

No.	Load Factor	Date
1.	89.9%	3/1/82
2.	89.8%	2/1/72
3.	89.7%	28/11/82
4.	88.5%	30/11/86
5.	88.5%	22/4/79

Above and below: *Two views of N128AA, a McDonnell Douglas DC-10-10 taking-off. This aircraft carries three crew members and anything between 237 and 290 passengers depending on seat configuration.* Austin J. Brown

Top Ten Markets For 1995.

No:	Market	Average Daily Passengers
1.	Los Angeles–New York	3,146
2.	Los Angeles–Dallas/Fort Worth	6,297
3.	Los Angeles–Chicago	3,533
4.	New York–San Juan	3,691
5.	New York–Dallas/Fort Worth	4,105
6.	New York–London	1,597
7.	Los Angeles–Miami	1,509
8.	Chicago–London	877
9.	New York–San Francisco	1,299
10.	Dallas/Fort Worth–Honolulu	858

Operating Information

AA Cities Served	189	AA Daily Departures	2,200
AMR Eagle Cities Served	160	AMR Eagle Daily Departures	1,500
Total	349	Total	3,700
AA Jet Fleet	637	AMR Eagle	208

Below: *The first of American's 767-223ERs was delivered in November 1985. It carries 166 passengers plus two or three flight crew.* Austin J. Brown